THAI
COOKING

JUDY WILLIAMS

THAI COOKING

Love Food ® is an imprint of Parragon Books Ltd

Parragon
Queen Street House
4 Queen Street
Bath BA1 1HE, UK

Created and produced by The Bridgewater Book Company Ltd.
Photography David Jordan
Home Economist Judy Williams
Location photography Kim Sayer, Simon Punter

ISBN: 978-1-4075-4923-1
Printed in China

NOTES FOR THE READER

• This book uses imperial, metric, or US cup measurements. Follow the same
units of measurement throughout; do not mix imperial and metric.

• All spoon measurements are level: teaspoons are assumed to be 5 ml, and
tablespoons are assumed to be 15 ml.

• Unless otherwise stated, milk is assumed to be whole, eggs and individual
vegetables such as potatoes are medium, and pepper is freshly ground
black pepper.

• Recipes using raw or very lightly cooked eggs should be avoided by infants,
the elderly, pregnant women, convalescents, and anyone with a chronic
condition.

• The times given are an approximate guide only. Preparation times differ
according to the techniques used by different people and the cooking times
may also vary from those given.

contents

Vegetarian Dishes (continued)

Main Meals 107

Stir-Fried Meals 147

Noodles & Rice 169

Noodles & Rice (continued)

Salads   197

Desserts   233

Index   254

INTRODUCTION

Welcome to Thailand or, rather, to a taste of it in your own home. Much as we would all like to go there, it's not always possible, so this is a taste of what it would be like, but without the long flight. In this Thailand, you have to do the cooking yourself; but don't worry, Thai cuisine is easy to tackle, the results are stunning, and the taste is wonderfully distinctive. You'll master the basics easily and soon be able to impress your friends and family.

The main problem used to be finding the ingredients, but with everyone traveling, reading, and eating out more we have all become increasingly ambitious and experimental in our cooking. Consequently, smaller more specialist stores as well as supermarkets have had to meet this need, and our stores are now full of lemon grass, chiles, galangal, and coconut milk. Although most ingredients are readily available, we have offered an alternative for the things that are trickier to find, such as jaggery and Thai basil (see pages 32–3).

Having been largely unexplored by Westerners for much of its past, Thailand is now one of the most popular places to visit, and with that interest comes a fascination for the food. Set between China and India, the flavors and tastes of those two countries have had an influence on Thai food, especially as the first settlers are thought to have come from southern China. It was they who introduced the techniques of stir-frying and steaming that have now become vital parts of Thai cooking.

Until 1939, Thailand was called Siam. Its ancient capital was Sukhothai, meaning "dawn of happiness" in Sanskrit. The country has seen many battles, and frequent changes of rulers, each bringing their own forms of government, language, and religion. Under the influential eye of King Ramkhamhaeng, the fabulously beautiful curly Thai alphabet was designed,

Buddhist art was created, and the cuisine and culture developed. Ayuthaya became a new capital, superseding Sukhothai in the mid-14th century and, after two hundred years of fighting and change, it was, in turn, destroyed. Its replacement, Thonburi, was founded as a royal capital in 1782 on the site that is now Bangkok.

Regional cuisine

Thailand is bordered by Malaysia, Myanmar (formerly Burma), Laos, and Cambodia. The flat central plains that lead to the Chao Phraya estuary are ideal for rice growing, much of which is exported. The northeast of the country is made up of the drier Khorat plateau, which slopes up to the mountains that include Doi Inthanon, the highest peak in Thailand. The east coastline runs for 930 miles/1,500 km from Trat province to the Malaysian border along the Gulf of Thailand. The west coastline down the peninsula runs 348 miles/560 km along the Andaman Sea from Rahong to Satun, past Phuket, a very popular holiday destination. There are also a great number of islands dotted along the coast.

There are three main seasons. The warmest period is from March to May. June to October is the rainy

Thailand is a place of distinct seasons, with June heralding a time of humidity and heavy rains

season, when it pours for a while each day, leaving a warm and humid atmosphere. The coolest time is from November to February. During these months the mountainous north gets much colder.

Obviously the varying topography, soils, and climate combine to determine which crops can be grown in the different regions and, although certain recipes are traditional wherever you are in Thailand, there may be subtle, local twists of flavors and ingredients. The country appears to divide into four main areas, each of which has its own particular style of cooking and eating.

The north of Thailand is full of interesting ruins and temples. This region was on the route from the East to the West taken by some of the earliest trading travelers. It was the most easily conquered part, adapting and changing when wars and battles took place. It is also the region that, allegedly, produces most of the country's opium.

The people of the north use more steamed, sticky, and glutinous rice and their curries are generally thinner in texture, as coconut milk is not used in their cooking. The influences of Myanmar and Laos can be seen in some of the curry dishes. Buffalo and pork are the main meats and I have heard that buffalo placenta is a highly desirable treat!

The northeast is the poorest and most infertile of Thailand's four regions. Droughts and other natural disasters have had an effect on its regional dishes. Ingredients such as meat and coconut are replaced with delicacies including grasshoppers, snails, and ants' eggs. Cooks have obviously had to be creative and inventive because the local produce is far less abundant but, as the country has developed, they are

Left *Hot chiles grow widely in Thailand's poorer northeast, and consequently feature heavily in the local dishes*

Overleaf *Bankok's floating market*

better able to source more interesting and useful ingredients. However, rice, the staple of Thai cuisine, has been growing in this part of the country since 4000 BC, when China was still growing and eating millet. Luckily, there are plenty of chiles grown in this part of Thailand—the locals like their food hot and consequently use a lot of them.

Southern Thailand is a long peninsula and has the advantage of the dense, central rainforest and lush climate as well as two coastlines. There are plenty of palm plantations, so coconut milk and jaggery feature in many of the dishes. The proximity of the sea means an abundance of fish and shellfish, from shrimp and scallops to squid and lobster, so many local recipes include these ingredients. They also produce crops of cashews, pineapple, and other fruits, such as pomelo.

The flat central plains are packed with vegetable gardens, paddy fields, and orchards, which, in turn, means that local produce is of high quality and incredibly plentiful. Most of the rice eaten in Thailand is grown here with more than half the country's revenue coming from its export. There are many ceremonies connected with the planting, growing, and harvesting of rice in appreciation of it, especially around Songkran—the Thai New Year. This occurs in mid-April, lasts for three days and marks the sun's moving from Aries into Taurus. Lots of water is thrown round during this celebration to symbolize cleansing and renewal. Buddha is cleaned as a mark of respect and as a blessing from the older people to the younger generation. Plenty of fun is had at the same time.

Abundant rice and the variety of fresh fruit and vegetables mean a wide assortment of dishes are prepared. The four large cities in Thailand, including Bangkok, are situated in this area, so there are huge numbers of people to cater for and feed.

One way most Western visitors get their taste

and knowledge of Thai food is from the throngs of specialist street stalls in the main cities. Hawkers have their own portable small stalls in which they carry round their tools, ingredients, and means of cooking. Bangkok also has a floating market, with long, thin boats, packed with fresh or cooked foods. Entire families can be seen traveling in these boats, crouching on the bottom or perched on sacks, while the cooking is done over a small charcoal or gas burner.

For many young people packing their rucksacks and trekking off round the world today, Thailand seems to be the place to start. The Khao San Road in Bangkok is often the backpacker's first stop for a taste of real Thai food for very little outlay. Traditionally, hawkers sold freshly cooked noodles,

The flat central plains are packed with vegetable gardens, paddy fields, and orchards...local produce is of high quality and incredibly plentiful

but their repertoire may now include bowls of steaming soup, barbecued meats, sticky rice, and banana crêpes—perfect for hungry travelers and city workers alike. The hustle and bustle of these street markets is very much a way of life for the huge crush of people who live and work in the large cities. However, away from these large tourist attractions, Thai people stick to a more traditional diet. Cooking for visitors is very different from the everyday meals that are eaten at home. Few Thai people use recipe books. They have learned by watching their families cook and it is very much a "cook, taste and add a little more" style of cooking.

Chinese food stores...are filled with ingredients that we're often barely able to recognize, let alone know how to cook

Buying and storing

Until recently, refrigerators were not common in Thailand and consequently, many Thai people shop daily. Shopping is usually done in the morning and the food is cooked the same day. However, all the usual, sensible rules about cooking, storing food, chilling, and freezing still apply to Thai cooking. As Westerners are more likely to shop weekly, we need to ensure that the ingredients we use are the best on the day of purchase if we're not going to eat the food for 3–4 days. Use only fresh produce and keep it chilled until required. Check the "best-before" and "use-by" date stamps and be extra careful when buying fish and shellfish, as these should be eaten on the day of purchase or frozen immediately—but only if they haven't been frozen before.

Some Thai dishes, such as vegetable curries, can be prepared the day before if they are slightly under-cooked, cooled, and then stored in the refrigerator. This gives the seasonings a chance to develop and mature, so the final curry will have a greater depth of flavor, and the vegetables do not fall apart or become too soggy to taste good when reheated.

For the same reasons, you may also want to undercook slightly a meal that you intend to freeze. Freezing also degrades flavor and texture, so again vegetables will be softer and blander. Meat dishes, especially chicken, however, must be thoroughly cooked prior to chilling or freezing. Make sure the dish is cold, pack it into a freezerproof container or bag, date and label it clearly, and freeze for no longer than three months. Don't forget that food

Left *Kaffir limes yield little juice but are very full flavored*

Overleaf *Many agricultural tasks are carried out manually*

should never be frozen for a second time. Rice, on the other hand, is best eaten on the day of cooking. Leftover rice can be kept in the fridge overnight but discarded if not used the next day. Chill food only once it is cold and cover dishes with plastic wrap. The aromas may penetrate everything else in the fridge and who wants to drink milk or orange juice when it has a tang of chiles and cilantro!

Sourcing ingredients

Large supermarkets stock a range of sauces, noodles, dried mushrooms, chili sauces, curry pastes, coconut milk, and many of the herbs and spices needed for Thai cooking. There will always be a few things that are hard to find and specialist Chinese food stores are often the place to hunt down these items. These stores are filled with ingredients that we're often barely able to recognize, let alone know how to cook, and they also have a strange, exotic smell. Asking what foods are, how to prepare them and then experimenting with them are great ways of getting to know Thai food. Nevertheless, with a simple recipe to follow and the determination to succeed, you will soon get to grips with the art of Thai cooking.

Equipment

You need at least three good cutting boards, one for meat, one for vegetables and herbs, and a third for fish. Scrub them clean before and after use, especially meat and fish boards. Most people use plastic, which is dishwashersafe and can be sterilized, rather than wood or marble for fish and meat.

Knives need to be varied in size—large blades for chopping herbs and slicing meat and fish, small ones for preparing vegetables.

The most important piece of equipment is the wok. All types of food—curries and soups, stir-fries and noodles—may be cooked in it

Above and opposite *Paying their respects to images of Buddha is part of daily life for the majority of Thai people*

Overleaf *River plains provide the most fertile farming soil*

A mortar and pestle is traditional, but many cooks prefer the easier, faster option of a food processor, with a blender and a small grinder for chopping, grinding, and puréeing ingredients, processing fish for fish cakes, and making curry pastes.

Probably the most important piece of equipment is the wok. All types of food—curries and soups, stir-fries and noodles—may be cooked in it. It is routinely used for deep-frying in Thailand. You can buy a two-handled wok, but I prefer the version with one wooden handle: it doesn't get so hot.

The traditional steel wok needs seasoning before use as it is sold with a protective oiled coating to prevent it from rusting. Scrub off the coating in warm soapy water, rinse well, and half dry. Stand the damp wok on a stove over low heat until it is dry. Drizzle a little oil into the wok and wipe it round the inside with a piece of paper towel. Continue heating gently until the oil smokes and burns off, then repeat with another coating of oil. The wok will darken in color and should never be scrubbed again, just wiped carefully. If food sticks or burns and the wok does need scrubbing, it will probably need to be seasoned again. All steel woks are sold with the manufacturer's instructions, so read through before using for the first time.

Nonstick woks are also available, usually from supermarkets and department stores. These won't rust, don't need oiling, and can be washed up like other pans. Check if they are dishwashersafe.

Other tools include the usual assortment of spatulas, slotted spoons, measuring cup, and spoons, a vegetable peeler, a garlic press, a whisk, and so on. You also need a steamer for dumplings and egg rolls. Bamboo steamers, placed over a wok of simmering

As a rule, Thais eat three meals a day and at least two of those will include rice

water, are favored by both Thai and Chinese cooks. If you opt to use a metal steamer or colander, it needs to be flat-bottomed, rather than one with sloping sides. This type is great for draining and steaming small quantities of vegetables, but you need a flat bottom on which to arrange small packages of food so that they cook evenly. Ensure the steamer fits tightly over the wok or pan of simmering water or most of the steam will escape round the edges.

A useful tool that is fun to learn to use is the cleaver. It looks unbelievably heavy and awkward, but once you get used to the weight and the fact that it's very sharp, it is an amazingly versatile piece of equipment—excellent for cutting thicker pieces of meat, as well as finely chopping onions or garlic. That will really make you feel like a proper Thai chef.

Thai meals

As a rule, Thais eat three meals a day and at least two of those will include rice. Breakfast might be some sort of rice-based soup and city workers might stop for noodles at lunchtime from one of the street hawkers. A traditional dinner, maybe in the company of guests, will be the main meal of the day. Several curries will be cooked and served, perhaps with a salad and some vegetable dishes. This main Thai meal will also be accompanied by rice. Thai people are not worried about eating food hot—it is often served either warm or at room temperature. They eat mainly with a spoon and fork, not chopsticks, using the fork to load the spoon, although chopsticks are more popular when eating noodles. Dessert may be one of a delicious range using such ingredients as mung bean flour and fruit to make cakes, or coconut milk with sliced fruit to make jellies.

Preparation

So, now that we have a better understanding of Thai food, let's get on with cooking some of the fabulous, varied ingredients that identify the cuisine. Thai-style cooking is now very popular in the West because it is so quick, but you do need to spend time beforehand on preparation.

Do read the recipe thoroughly and have all the ingredients ready. Prepare and chop all the chiles, ginger, vegetables etc. Ensure you have Thai fish sauce to hand and enough oil to deep-fry those shrimp. Do check the method too, as it's a nuisance to find you should have peeled the tomatoes before adding them to the dish and there they are, pristine, whole, with their skins firmly on. (*For reference: use a sharp knife to mark a cross on the base of each tomato, place in a bowl, and cover with boiling water. Leave for 5 minutes, rinse in water, and peel off the skins. Quarter, seed, and chop the flesh.*) I do give weights of vegetables but you will know how much you and/or your family will eat and can adjust quantities accordingly. Everything should be flexible, so if in doubt about the heat of a curry paste, add half the quantity, cook, and taste. Equally, if you are only cooking for two, halve the quantities; for more than four, increase them accordingly. Be creative in how you use the recipes—but do be sure to stick to either imperial or metric measurements.

Eating Thai food is an amazing experience because the flavors are such a marvelous mixture of hot, sweet, and sour. The taste is astringent, leaving your teeth feeling clean and your mouth alive. In most people's opinion, chile is the key ingredient in Thai cooking. It is used in most savory recipes, freshly chopped or blended into a paste. Yet the secret is less about heat, rather the harmony derived from the delicate taste and fragrance of coconut milk, lemon grass, galangal, kaffir lime leaves, jaggery, and Thai fish sauce—the quintessential elements of Thai food. So, on with the recipes and, please, relax and enjoy the experience. Cooking is meant to be fun and this book is certainly about just that.

Noodles

Rice is Thailand's main staple, but noodles run it a close second and, in some ways, noodle dishes typify the very essence of Thai cuisine. Variety—in flavor and texture—is the keynote and noodle dishes are almost infinitely diverse. Noodles may be combined with any number of other ingredients, including meat, poultry, fish, seafood, vegetables, and the ubiquitous chile. They are served hot or cold, in soups and salads, deep-fried or stir-fried, braised or shaped into attractive little nests. A noodle dish may be one of several different dishes—all of equal importance—served as part of a family meal. Equally, a steaming bowl of freshly cooked noodles tossed in a flavorsome sauce makes a welcome mid-morning snack or a tasty treat bought from a roadside stall late in the evening.

The versatility of noodle dishes is further extended by the wide variety of types available. Rice noodles, which range in thickness from thin strands to flat ribbons, are the most popular. Fried with seafood, tofu, vegetables, and a selection of sauces, they could be described as Thailand's national dish. Dried rice noodles are sold in bundles and are usually soaked in warm water as a preliminary to further cooking. You will find fresh rice noodles in specialist stores and some supermarkets. Egg noodles, familiar

The busy, colorful markets are the place to buy the freshest spices, fruits, and vegetables that provide the keynote flavors to Thailand's cooking

Noodles may be combined with any number of other ingredients...meat, poultry, fish, seafood, vegetables

from Chinese cooking, are also widely used in Thailand. These are made from wheat flour, egg, and water and come in a variety of shapes and sizes. Usually they are cooked in boiling water and may then be added to soups or stir-fries toward the end of cooking. Boiled and very thoroughly drained, they can also be fried to make crisp noodle cakes.

Cellophane noodles, also known as bean thread, glass, or transparent noodles, are made from ground mung beans. They must be soaked to soften them and can then be added to stir-fries, curries, and they are a favorite for salads. Rice vermicelli are very thin, rather brittle noodles, usually sold in somewhat unwieldy bundles. Once soaked, they cook almost instantly in water, stock, or coconut milk. They can also be deep-fried, creating wonderful tangled nests. Crisp-fried rice vermicelli, combined with pork, shrimp, and vegetables and tossed in a piquant sweet-and-sour sauce, is a popular special-occasion dish known as *mee krob*.

Noodles are not hard to cook, but timing is critical as they can quickly become sodden and unappetizing. Check the package instructions for the recommended cooking time. Take especial care when precooking noodles before stir-frying, deep-frying, or adding to soups. Remove them from the heat as soon as they are just tender, drain thoroughly, and then refresh under cold running water to prevent further cooking. Drain well again, particularly if they are to be fried.

Dried noodles may be kept for months in an air-tight container. Keep fresh noodles for several days in the refrigerator but do check the "use-by" date.

Rice

Every Thai person probably eats about 1 lb 2 oz/500 g of rice a day, whether in the form of noodles or as plain rice, for breakfast, lunch, or dinner. It certainly seems to be the main staple, owing much to the fact that no wheat grows in Thailand. The Thais also use rice flour, which has a very distinctive texture, to thicken their sauces and curries, sometimes to dust meat that is to be stir-fried or to bind meat and other ingredients together.

A large bowl of rice forms the centerpiece on a Thai family table, surrounded with vegetable, fish, meat, and other curry dishes. The Thais never serve rice as an accompaniment to a main dish.

Rice dishes, as well as noodles, can easily be bought from the hawkers and various vendors that fill the streets in cities such as Bangkok and Chiengmai. Popular dishes include coconut rice, egg-fried rice, and hot, spicy rice.

There are two main types of rice in Thailand. In the north and northeast, a sticky, glutinous, short-grain variety is preferred, often eaten with the fingers. Because of its texture, the rice can be rolled into balls and then dipped into sweet or savory sauces and condiments. Glutinous rice is usually soaked before steaming. You should not rinse it more than twice, otherwise you will wash off all the starch that makes it sticky.

The second type of rice, a long-grain variety, is the fluffy, fragrant rice, such as jasmine and basmati, which is often more popular in the Western world than the glutinous. Fragrant rice can be boiled or steamed and then sometimes fried. It is important that you don't overcook rice, or it will become stodgy and bland. There should always be twice as much water as rice. The easiest way to tell whether it is cooked is to bite a grain between your front teeth. Alternatively, press a grain between your finger and thumb: it should break into three pieces.

Remember to experiment with your rice dishes; this is, after all, what Thai cooking in this book is all about. Use a mix-and-match method and devise your own creations by combining different flavorings. Try throwing a couple of lime leaves, some chile, grated coconut, or a lemon grass stalk in with the rice while it is cooking—just remember to take out the leaves or lemon grass before you serve it.

Rice is also used for desserts and candies. Short-grain rice can be turned into a special Spicy Rice Pudding (see page 240) for a sweet and spicy Thai treat. To make rice crackers Thai cooks deliberately leave a crisp layer of rice on the bottom of the pan in which it has been cooked, then remove it and put it in the sun to dry. The crisp pieces are fried in hot oil and dipped in syrup or coconut.

Cooking rice

People are often worried about cooking rice, thinking that it always sticks and goes clumpy, but this is only when it is overcooked. Check package instructions and follow them for perfect rice every time.

Sticky, glutinous rice needs to be soaked overnight and then steamed for 8-10 minutes, until tender. It can then be eaten hot or packed into a container, leveled off, and chilled. The resulting slab can be cut into small square rice cakes that are often served with satay dishes.

There are several different ways of cooking jasmine or other long-grain rice and opinions differ as to which is best. The first way is to put the rice into a measuring cup, up to the level of ½ cup per person. Wash it and then tip into a pan. Measure double the volume of water and pour it into the pan. Bring to a boil, reduce the heat, cover, and let simmer very gently for 12–15 minutes, without stirring or disturbing it. Turn off the heat and leave, covered, for 3–4 minutes before serving. A second method is to put the rinsed rice into a pan and add water to

cover it by about 1 inch/2.5 cm, or the distance to the first knuckle on your index finger. Add a pinch of salt, cover, bring to a boil and let simmer for 1–2 minutes, then turn off the heat and leave in the pan, covered, for 25 minutes. The water should have been absorbed; the rice should be fluffy and ready to eat.

Other people prefer the easy option and use the boil-in-the-bag variety. But cooking ordinary rice isn't tricky at all and once you have found the method that suits you, rice will be on the menu more often.

Curry pastes

We've all eyed up the colorful rows of curry pastes lining the shelves in the supermarkets, ready-made for our convenience, and do use them if you want to. There's nothing wrong with that. The authentic ones save time and effort chopping what seems like hundreds of chiles, and all the cleaning and washing up. However, it is more fun to have a go yourself. It also means the flavors will be fresher and taste cleaner and stronger, and, without doubt, homemade curry pastes beat the bottled versions hands down. Do use good-quality, fresh ingredients, as the final product will last longer and taste better.

There are several types of curry paste and although the basic ingredients are similar, they all add a different flavor and degree of heat to the recipe. It is also helpful to understand how they vary and why, and at least you'll know whether to pick a yellow, red or green curry next time you're dining in a Thai restaurant. Thai green curry is the hottest. This is because the Green Curry Paste calls for small, hot fresh green chiles, not dried ones. Red Curry Paste

Overleaf *Tending the all-important paddy fields in the country's great central plains is back-breaking work for Thailand's rice farmers*

There are several types of curry paste, and, although the basic ingredients are similar, they all add a different flavor and degree of heat to the recipe

is milder, as it usually uses dried red chiles, and Yellow Curry Paste (see page 93) is the mildest. There is also a Penang Curry Paste (page 114), which has a Malaysian influence, and the famous Mussaman Curry Paste (page 124) is a favorite with Thai Muslims and is much more like an Indian flavoring.

So, get out your cutting board and sharp knives, and rubber gloves for preparing the chiles, unless, like me, you use a sharp knife and fork to avoid handling them. You'll need a blender, food processor, a grinder, or mortar and pestle to make pastes, and a wok or large skillet.

curry paste recipes

Green Curry Paste

1 tbsp coriander seeds

1 tbsp cumin seeds

1 tsp shrimp paste

15 fresh green Thai chiles, chopped

2 shallots, chopped

6 garlic cloves, chopped

1-inch/2.5-cm piece of fresh galangal, chopped

2 lemon grass stalks (white part only), chopped

6 kaffir lime leaves, chopped

2 tbsp chopped cilantro root

grated rind of 1 lime

1 tsp salt

1 tsp black peppercorns

Red Curry Paste

1 tbsp coriander seeds

1 tbsp cumin seeds

2 tsp shrimp paste

12 dried or fresh red chiles, chopped

2 shallots, chopped

8 garlic cloves, chopped

1-inch/2.5-cm piece of fresh galangal, chopped

2 lemon grass stalks (white part only), chopped

4 kaffir lime leaves, chopped

2 tbsp chopped cilantro root

grated rind of 1 lime

1 tsp black peppercorns

Dry-fry the coriander and cumin seeds in a heavy-bottom skillet, stirring constantly, for 2–3 minutes, until browned. Remove from the heat and grind to a powder with a mortar and pestle or spice grinder, or process in a blender.

Wrap the shrimp paste in a piece of foil and broil or dry-fry for 2–3 minutes, turning once or twice. Put the ground spices, shrimp paste, and chiles into a blender or food processor and process until finely chopped. Add the remaining ingredients and process again to a smooth paste, scraping down the sides as necessary.

Young members of a farming family will often be required to help with the daily task of selling their produce in the local markets

In the Thai kitchen

Bean sprouts These are usually sprouted mung beans, but many other beans can be sprouted. They need to be used quickly, as they soon deteriorate. Added at the last minute, they give crunch and a nutty flavor.

Cardamom These small, hard seeds are sold in the pod and used whole to add a spicy taste to stocks, curries, even ice cream. Ground seeds are used in curry pastes.

Chiles The most-used chiles are red or green—the orange and yellow ones only represent different stages of ripeness. Large smooth chiles are usually milder. Longer, thinner, knobbly ones are hotter and the very small Thai chiles are fiery hot. Cutting out most of the membrane with the seeds removes a lot of the heat but not the flavor. Use rubber gloves to protect your fingers and don't rub your eyes! The leaves are often used as a vegetable; hot or sweet **chili sauces** served as an accompaniment.

Chinese dried mushrooms Assorted dried mushrooms are now more widely available in the West. They need soaking in hot water before use. The stalks on larger, whole mushrooms are tough and should be discarded. The soaking water is often added to the dish as well, but may need to be diluted as it can be very strong.

Chinese or garlic chives are longer and flatter than Western ones, often sold with their flowers attached. Use them chopped or whole as a garnish, or steamed whole for 1–2 minutes for tying tiny food packages.

Choy sum or Chinese flowering cabbage has long stems and leaves with pretty yellow flowers. Use in the same way as **Broccoli**—both are full of goodness—especially in stir-fries. Don't overcook: it turns gray and soggy, loses its vitamins, and tastes horrible.

Cilantro Fresh cilantro is an essential ingredient in Thai cuisine. The roots are used in sauces or marinades; the leaves chopped and stirred into sauces during cooking or sprinkled as a garnish and a flavoring.

Coconut Probably the best-known ingredient in Thai cooking. Canned coconut milk is usually half solid and half liquid. Creamed coconut comes in solid blocks. Dry unsweetened coconut needs reconstituting with hot water. To make a thick creamy coconut sauce, use ¾ cup dry unsweetened coconut to generous ¾ cup water. For a thinner sauce, mix ½ cup dry unsweetened coconut with generous 1 cup hot water.

Cumin These seeds can be added to hot oil to flavor it before cooking starts. They are also dry-fried in curry paste recipes. Whole seeds and ground cumin are easily found in supermarkets and food stores.

Curry pastes and sauces Thai curries are thinner and more fragrant than Indian ones. Homemade curry pastes take time to make; prepared pastes are quick and easy, and usually come marked with degrees of heat. Always add them gradually, especially if you don't like your food too spicy. Ready-made curry sauces are less concentrated than the pastes. For an instant meal, pour them over noodles or toss in rice.

Egg roll skins These square dough skins come ready for use in packages of about 20. Leftover sheets can be frozen for another time. Handle them carefully. Keep covered with a damp dish towel or plastic wrap until ready to use, as they dry out quickly.

Fish sauce Made from small fish and shrimp that have been fermented in the sun, this salty, thin, brown sauce is an essential part of Thai cooking. Most recipes—and not only fish ones—include it in small quantities (the flavor is very intense).

Galangal Similar in taste to ginger but subtler in flavor. Used in soups, curries, and spice pastes. The fresh peeled root can be sliced or grated; in its dried form galangal must be soaked to reconstitute. Galangal is also sold grated or sliced in jars.

Garlic Used in almost all savory Thai recipes, usually added at the start, often stir-fried with onion.

Ginger Peppery-hot and refreshing, ginger plays a major part in Thai cooking. A fresh root is pink. Blue or gray edges indicate that it is stale and too fibrous.

Jaggery Derived from the flower of the palm tree. It varies in color and is less sweet than cane or beet sugar. It comes in a block that can be crumbled or melted. Use soft, light brown sugar as an alternative.

Lemon grass The tough stalks of this grass are snapped into pieces and added to soups or stocks. For curry pastes, only the finely chopped inner white part is used. The stalks can be frozen and used as required.

Limes and lime leaves Although common limes can be used, smaller kaffir limes are more familiar in Thailand. The thick rind is full of flavor but there is almost no juice. They can be eaten if chopped small, but discard them if using whole. The leaves add an astringent flavor to stocks, soups, and curries.

Magic paste Use a bulb of garlic, peeled and ground with a bunch of fresh cilantro leaves and roots, and ¼ cup white peppercorns. Keep in the fridge for 3–4 days or freeze in small amounts. It is also sold in jars.

Napa cabbage is a long, pale, densely packed vegetable with frilly leaves. Shred it and add toward the end of cooking so that it remains crunchy, or use in salads. Sold pickled and canned, for use as a side dish.

Oils Most cooking in Thailand uses palm oil, as it is in plentiful supply and flavorless. You can use vegetable oil, but olive oil cannot be heated to stir-frying temperature and is too strong. Sesame oil may be used sparingly, more for flavor, or in marinades.

Rice flour A fine white flour used to thicken soups and bind meaty mixtures. Cornstarch is a substitute.

Shrimp paste A thick paste with a very strong smell made from dried salted shrimp. Use in small amounts, as its flavor is very intense. It must be cooked before using but doesn't need to be stored in the refrigerator once opened. Tiny salted **dried shrimp** may be found in Chinese food stores. They need to be ground or processed and are then added to pastes and sauces.

Thai basil or holy basil leaves are thinner and flimsier than the more familiar basil used in Italian cooking. Thai basil has a mild aniseed flavor, a lovely smell and adds a fantastic flavor to curries and soups, but substitute common basil if you can't get the Thai one.

Tofu Made from solid bean curd—highly nutritious and incredibly versatile as it readily absorbs flavors. The most useful is the firm white tofu that comes packaged in its own liquid. Use it as it is or, far tastier, cut into cubes, deep-fry, and add to curries and stir-fries. Ready-fried tofu is also sold.

Won ton skins Square dough sheets, rather like small egg roll skins, are made from wheat flour and egg. They can be steamed for a softer package and deep-fried for a crispy one.

Yard-long beans or snake beans Stringless beans which add little flavor, but extra crunch to curries and stir-fries.

APPETIZERS

Thai people don't really eat appetizers. Small portions of each dish—rice, curries, and salads—are served on plates or in bowls and eaten together, either with a spoon and fork or just with the fingers. However, in the West meals are generally separated into courses, so we have to adjust the recipes here to suit this custom.

Among the selection of recipes here to be served as appetizers you will find there are quite a lot of finger foods, which are served warm, and should be picked up, dunked into a tasty dip, and eaten immediately. There are other dishes that might need a spoon and fork, as they are quite soupy or involve eating rice or noodles.

The wok really is a most useful piece of equipment. Because it is deep as well as wide, it can be used for cooking everything, whether it is stir-fried vegetables with tofu or deep-fried won tons. Alternatively, if you don't possess one, you will need a large skillet or heavy-bottom pan for these recipes. These do need to be large ones, as you will need plenty of room to toss food, mix and stir-fry vegetables, or brown pieces of meat or fish. (You also could use a deep-fat fryer, but do make sure the oil is clear, light, and clean. Once it has turned dark, it should be changed. This is important as it will affect the flavor of, say, egg rolls if the last thing you cooked in your fryer was battered fish.)

Deep-fried food can be very greasy. Probably all of us have bitten into an egg roll only to have hot oil pour out, burn our chins, and spoil our clothes, so take care to put all fried foods on paper towels and pat well with more paper towels to remove as much of the oil as possible. An off-putting greasy texture and taste will also overpower the delicate flavor of the filling in a deep-fried package, whether

won ton or egg roll, or a crispy battered shrimp. If the oil is still fairly new and clean, but full of bits of batter or seeds, you can filter it. Let the oil cool completely first. Line a strainer with a double layer of paper towel and stand over a deep bowl. Gradually pour the cold oil into the strainer—it won't all fit at once—and filter it through the paper and into the bowl below. Discard the paper towel and its contents and pour the oil back into the skillet or wok. You may be able to do this twice but after that the oil will need changing; as it gets darker and darker it will affect the flavor of the food.

Some dishes need to be cooked in batches, so put the cooked batch into a warm oven or under a hot broiler while you cook the next batch, or simply

Appetizers are a way of stimulating the appetite rather than satisfying it. Your guests should be left feeling they could eat that all over again

cover with foil and keep on top of the oven. Since most of these appetizers are cooked quite quickly in hot oil, they don't cool down very fast. In any case, if you adopt the Thai style of eating, food is usually served lukewarm, rather than hot. Serve small portions because, although they may not look much, remember there are two more courses to follow. Appetizers are a way of stimulating the appetite rather than satisfying it. Your guests should be left feeling they could eat that all over again and knowing that there is even better to come.

Whatever you choose, remember that the job of the appetizer is to set the taste buds alight for the next course.

corn fritters
khao ped chup pang

SERVES 4

for the fritters

3 scallions, chopped finely

11¹/₂ oz/325 g canned corn kernels, drained

1 red bell pepper, seeded and finely chopped

small handful of fresh cilantro, chopped

2 garlic cloves, crushed

2 eggs

2 tsp superfine sugar

1 tbsp fish sauce

2 tbsp rice flour or cornstarch

vegetable or peanut oil, for pan-frying

for the dip

2 red bell peppers, seeded and halved

2 tomatoes, peeled, seeded, and chopped coarsely

1 tbsp vegetable or peanut oil, for pan-frying

1 onion, chopped

1 tbsp Red Curry Paste (see page 31)

3–4 sprigs fresh cilantro, chopped

1 Combine all the ingredients for the fritters in a bowl. Heat the oil in a skillet and cook spoonfuls of the mixture, in batches, until golden brown on the underside. Flip over with a spatula to cook the second side. Remove from the skillet, drain on paper towels, and keep warm.

2 To make the dip, put the red bell peppers on a baking sheet and place, skin-side up, under a hot broiler, until blackened. Using tongs, transfer to a plastic bag, tie the top, and let cool slightly.

3 When the bell peppers are cool enough to handle, peel off the skins, and chop the flesh. Put into a blender or food processor with the tomatoes and process until smooth.

4 Heat the oil in a heavy-bottom pan and cook the onion and curry paste for 3–4 minutes, until softened. Add the bell pepper and tomato purée and cook gently until tender and hot. Stir in the chopped cilantro, cook for 1 minute, and serve hot with the fritters.

won tons
kaeow

SERVES 4

for the filling

2 tbsp vegetable or peanut oil

6 scallions, chopped

4¹/₂ oz/125 g mushrooms, chopped

2 oz/55 g fine green beans, chopped

2 oz/55 g corn kernels, drained if canned

1 egg, beaten

3 tbsp Thai soy sauce

1 tbsp jaggery or soft, light brown sugar

¹/₂ tsp salt

for the won tons

24 won ton skins

1 egg, beaten

vegetable or peanut oil, for deep-frying

plum or chili sauce, to serve

1 To make the filling, heat the oil in a preheated
wok and stir-fry the scallions, mushrooms,
and beans for 1–2 minutes, until softened. Add the
corn, stir well to mix, and then push the vegetables to
the side. Pour in the egg. Stir until lightly set before
incorporating the vegetables and adding the soy sauce,
sugar, and salt. Remove the wok from the heat.

2 Place the won ton skins in a pile on a counter. Put
a teaspoonful of the filling in the center of the top
skin. Brush the edges with beaten egg and fold in half
diagonally to make a small triangular package. Repeat
with the remaining skins and filling.

3 Heat the oil for deep-frying in a wok or large
skillet. Add the packages, in batches, and deep-fry
for 3–4 minutes, until golden brown. Remove from the
wok with a slotted spoon and drain on paper towels.
Keep warm while you cook the remaining won tons.
Serve hot with plum or chili sauce.

crisp sesame shrimp
khung ob gha tord khob

SERVES 4

³/₄ cup self-rising flour

3 tbsp sesame seeds, toasted or dry-fried

1 tsp Red Curry Paste (see page 31)

1 tbsp fish sauce

²/₃ cup water

vegetable or peanut oil, for deep-frying

20 large uncooked shrimp, shelled with tails intact

chili sauce, for dipping

1 Combine the flour and sesame seeds in a bowl. Stir the curry paste, fish sauce, and water together in a pitcher until mixed. Gradually pour the liquid into the flour, stirring constantly, to make a thick batter.

2 Heat the oil for deep-frying in a wok or large skillet. Holding the shrimp by their tails, dip them into the batter, one at a time, then carefully drop into the hot oil. Cook for 2–3 minutes, until crisp and brown. Drain on paper towels and serve immediately with chili sauce.

1 Put the eggs, water, and Thai soy sauce in a bowl. Set aside. Mix together the scallions and chopped chile to form a paste.

2 Heat half the oil in an 8-inch/20-cm skillet and pour in half the egg mixture. Tilt to coat the bottom of the skillet evenly and cook until set. Lift out and set aside. Heat the remaining oil and make a second omelet in the same way.

3 Spread the scallion, chili paste, and curry paste in a thin layer over each omelet and sprinkle the cilantro on top. Roll up tightly. Cut each one in half and then cut each piece on the diagonal in half again. Serve immediately, while still warm.

omelet rolls
kai yud sai

SERVES 4

4 large eggs

2 tbsp water

1 tbsp Thai soy sauce

6 scallions, chopped finely

1 fresh red chile, seeded and chopped finely

1 tbsp vegetable or peanut oil

1 tbsp Green Curry Paste (see page 31)

bunch of fresh cilantro, chopped

fish cakes
thot man pla

SERVES 4

1 lb/450 g white fish fillets, skinned and cut into cubes

1 egg white

2 kaffir lime leaves, torn coarsely

1 tbsp Green Curry Paste (see page 31)

2 oz/55 g green beans, chopped finely

1 fresh red chile, seeded and chopped finely

bunch of fresh cilantro, chopped

vegetable or peanut oil for cooking

1 fresh green chile, seeded and sliced, to serve

for the dipping sauce

generous ½ cup superfine sugar

¼ cup white wine vinegar

1 small carrot, cut into thin sticks

2-inch/5-cm piece cucumber, peeled, seeded, and cut
   into thin sticks

1 Put the fish into a food processor with the egg white, lime leaves, and curry paste, and process until smooth. Scrape the mixture into a bowl and stir in the green beans, red chile, and cilantro.

2 With dampened hands, shape the mixture into small patties, about 2 inches/5 cm across. Place them on a large plate in a single layer and let chill for 30 minutes.

3 Meanwhile, make the dipping sauce. Put the sugar in a pan with 1½ tablespoons water and the vinegar and heat gently, stirring until the sugar has dissolved. Add the carrot and cucumber, then remove from the heat and let cool.

4 Heat the oil in a skillet and cook the fish cakes, in batches, until golden brown on both sides. Drain on paper towels and keep warm while you cook the remaining batches. If you like, reheat the dipping sauce. Serve the fish cakes immediately with warm or cold dipping sauce, topped with chile slices.

*Thai architecture is as colorful and
distinctive as the country's cuisine*

These taste great cooked under the broiler, but using the barbecue adds that extra smoky flavor.

chicken satay
satay gai

SERVES 4

2 tbsp vegetable or peanut oil

1 tbsp sesame oil

juice of ¹/₂ lime

2 skinned, boned chicken breasts, cut into
   small cubes

for the dip

2 tbsp vegetable or peanut oil

1 small onion, chopped finely

1 small fresh green chile, seeded and chopped

1 garlic clove, chopped finely

¹/₂ cup crunchy peanut butter

6–8 tbsp water

juice of ¹/₂ lime

1 Combine both the oils and the lime juice in a nonmetallic dish. Add the chicken cubes, cover with plastic wrap, and let chill for 1 hour.

2 To make the dip, heat the oil in a skillet and sauté the onion, chile, and garlic over low heat, stirring occasionally, for about 5 minutes, until just softened. Add the peanut butter, water, and lime juice and let simmer gently, stirring constantly, until the peanut butter has softened enough to make a dip—you may need to add extra water to make a thinner consistency.

3 Meanwhile, drain the chicken cubes and thread them onto 8–12 wooden skewers*. Put under a hot broiler or on a barbecue, turning frequently, for about 10 minutes, until cooked and browned. Serve hot with the warm dip.

*cook's tip
Soak wooden skewers in cold water for 45 minutes before threading the meat to help stop them burning during cooking.

Sculpture and intricate decoration are key elements of Thai art

beef stir-fry
pahd nuea

1 Heat the oil in a wok or large skillet and stir-fry the onions, garlic, and ginger for 1 minute. Add the beef strips and stir-fry over high heat until browned all over. Add the vegetables and the two pastes and cook for 2–3 minutes until blended and cooked.

2 Stir in the cilantro and basil and serve immediately with rice.

SERVES 4

2 tbsp vegetable or peanut oil

2 medium red onions, sliced thinly

2 garlic cloves, chopped

1-inch/2.5-cm piece gingerroot, cut into thin sticks

2 x 4 oz/115 g beef fillets, sliced thinly

1 green bell pepper, seeded and sliced

5$^{1}/_{2}$ oz/150 g canned bamboo shoots

$^{3}/_{4}$ cup bean sprouts

2 tbsp Magic Paste (see page 33)

1 tbsp Red Curry Paste (see page 31)

handful of fresh cilantro, chopped

few sprigs Thai basil

boiled rice, to serve

Overleaf *Any visitor to Thailand will be struck by the imposing gold statues of Buddha*

crispy egg rolls
po pia thot

SERVES 4

2 tbsp vegetable or peanut oil

6 scallions, cut into 2-inch/5-cm lengths

1 fresh green chile, seeded and chopped

1 carrot, cut into thin sticks

1 zucchini, cut into thin sticks

$^1/_2$ red bell pepper, seeded and thinly sliced

$^3/_4$ cup bean sprouts

4 oz/115 g canned bamboo shoots, drained and rinsed

3 tbsp Thai soy sauce

1–2 tbsp chili sauce

8 egg roll skins

vegetable or peanut oil, for deep-frying

1 Heat the oil in a wok and stir-fry the scallions and chile for 30 seconds. Add the carrot, zucchini, and red bell pepper and stir-fry for 1 minute more. Remove the wok from heat and stir in the bean sprouts, bamboo shoots, soy sauce, and chili sauce. Taste and add more soy sauce or chili sauce if necessary.

2 Place an egg roll skin on a counter and spoon some of the vegetable mixture diagonally across the center. Roll one corner over the filling and flip the sides of the skin over the top, to enclose the filling. Continue to roll up to make an enclosed package. Repeat with the remaining skins and filling to make 8 egg rolls.

3 Heat the oil for deep-frying in a wok or large skillet. Deep-fry the egg rolls, 3–4 at a time, until crisp and golden brown. Remove with a slotted spoon, drain on paper towels while you cook the remainder, then serve immediately.

crispy wrapped shrimp
khung hao tord khob

SERVES 4

16 large unpeeled cooked shrimp

juice of 1 lime

4 tbsp chili sauce

16 won ton skins

vegetable or peanut oil, for deep-frying

plum sauce, to serve

1 Remove the heads and shell the shrimp, but leave the tails intact. Place them in a nonmetallic bowl, add the lime juice, and toss lightly to coat. Set aside in a cool place for 30 minutes.

2 Spread a little chili sauce over a won ton skin. Place a shrimp diagonally across it, leaving the tail protruding. Fold the bottom corner of the skin over the shrimp, fold the next corner up over the head and then roll the shrimp up in the skin, so that the body is encased, but the tail is exposed. Repeat with the remaining skins, chili sauce, and shrimp.

3 Heat the oil in a wok or skillet and deep-fry the shrimp, in batches, until crisp and browned. Serve hot with plum sauce for dipping.

crab packages
pue hao

SERVES 4

12 oz/350 g canned white crabmeat, drained

1 fresh red chile, seeded and chopped

4 scallions, sliced finely

1 tbsp Red Curry Paste (see page 31)

juice of ¹/₂ lime

¹/₂ tsp salt

20 won ton skins

oil for cooking

for the dip

generous ¹/₄ cup superfine sugar

2 tbsp water

2 tbsp rice wine vinegar

3 pieces preserved ginger, sliced

1 tbsp ginger syrup from the jar

1 Put the crabmeat into a bowl and add the chile, onions, and curry paste. Stir together with the lime juice and salt.

2 Put the skins in a pile and put 1 portion of the crabmeat in the center of the top skin. Brush the edges with a little water and roll up the edges to make a small cigar-shaped package. Continue to make packages with the skins—you need at least 20.

3 Heat the oil in a wok or large skillet and cook the packages, a few at a time, until golden brown. Drain on paper towels.

4 Put all the ingredients for the dip in a small pan and heat gently until the sugar has melted. Serve warm with the crab packages.

*Rickshaws are commonly used to travel
short distances in Thailand*

lettuce wraps
puk hao

Make sure you have a plentiful supply of napkins ready when serving these tasty little packages.

SERVES 4

1 iceberg lettuce

1 tbsp vegetable or peanut oil

1 onion, chopped finely

1 fresh red chile, seeded and chopped

1$\frac{1}{2}$ cups ground pork

7 oz/200 g canned water chestnuts, drained, rinsed, and chopped

3–4 tbsp Thai soy sauce

1 tsp jaggery or soft, light brown sugar

1–2 tbsp Green Curry Paste (see page 31)

3–4 fresh Thai basil leaves, torn coarsely

1 Separate the lettuce leaves, wash well in cold water*, and shake dry. Place all the leaves upside down on a large plate and let chill for 2 hours.

2 Heat the oil in a wok and stir-fry the onion and chile for 30 seconds. Add the ground pork and stir-fry for 8–10 minutes, until browned and crisp. Stir in the water chestnuts, soy sauce, sugar, curry paste, and basil leaves, and cook for an additional 2–3 minutes.

3 Transfer the pork mixture to a warmed serving dish and serve immediately with the chilled lettuce leaves. Each guest can put a spoonful of the pork mixture into the center of a lettuce leaf, roll it up, and eat with their hands.

*cook's tip

To separate the lettuce leaves, cut off the stalk, and hold the lettuce under cold running water. As the water runs between the leaves the weight of it separates them without tearing.

steamed egg rolls
po pia nuag

SERVES 4

12 rice flour crêpes

12–24 fresh Thai basil leaves

2 tbsp chili sauce, plus extra for serving

24 cooked shelled jumbo shrimp

4 scallions, cut into thin strips

1 carrot, cut into thin sticks

2 oz/55 g rice vermicelli noodles, cooked and drained

1 Place the crêpes between 2 dampened dish towels and let stand for 2 minutes, until soft. Alternatively, soak them in warm water and lift out one at a time to work on.

2 Place 1–2 basil leaves in the center of a crêpe and top with a little chili sauce. Arrange 2 shrimp on top and then some of the scallions and carrot. Add a few noodles and roll up. Flip one edge of the crêpe over the filling, fold the sides over to enclose it, and roll up. Repeat with the remaining crêpes and filling.

3 Arrange the filled crêpes in a single layer in the top of a steamer. Cook over simmering water for 4–5 minutes, until heated through. Serve immediately with extra chili sauce for dipping.

SOUPS

Soups form a major part of any Thai meal and are served at the same time as all the other dishes. In the West, we think of them as an alternative to an appetizer, maybe a lunchtime snack, or plan to serve a really chunky soup as a main meal. Some soups can be very filling indeed, so you need to plan your menu carefully.

stir in herbs at the end, so they wilt and flavor the soup as they are gently incorporated into the liquid

A thin, watery soup with a few mushrooms and a little shredded chicken is definitely one to be served as an appetizer soup, designed to stimulate the taste buds and wake up the whole mouth ready for the second course. Other soups, such as Shrimp Laksa (see page 63), are thickened with coconut milk and contain noodles and so may be enough to satisfy a hungry person looking for a filling lunch.

Cooks in the West may be used to following the basic method for making soup of heating a little oil, lightly sautéing a mixture of vegetables and then adding stock, herbs, and seasonings. Thai soups, on the other hand, are often made with heated stock or coconut milk to which vegetables, meat, or fish are then added, so no sautéing is involved. This chapter includes recipes using both techniques. Some of them are made with a combination of Eastern and Western culinary styles and flavorings, while others are more traditional, but there is sure to be something for everyone.

Some of the recipes require stock as a base and, obviously, it is better if you can make your own. However, for the occasions when you don't have the time or inclination, a good-quality bouillon cube will still give perfectly good results. Those soups that are based on coconut milk, not stock, will be thicker, richer, and more filling. Cans of coconut milk are readily available from most large food stores, as well as specialist supermarkets. Shake the can vigorously

before opening it, or stir well once the lid is opened to incorporate the thinner, watery milk with the coconut cream—you need both.

Although soups are made in a wok in Thailand, you can use a pan. Choose one with a heavy bottom, if possible, especially for the thicker soups, to prevent the liquid from sticking and burning. Most soups are made with 3½–5 cups of liquid, but, before you start, check that your pan is large enough to accommodate all the ingredients— vegetables, meat, or fish and the liquid—and allow room for stirring as well. Cut your root vegetables to a similar size and they will cook in the same time; stir in herbs at the end so that they wilt and flavor the soup as they are gently incorporated into the liquid.

The wonderful aroma of the flavorings used in Thai soup is enough to make your mouth water

If you are adding rice and noodles to a soup, take care to make sure that when you put them in they will have the correct amount of time to cook. They continue to swell in the hot liquid and both will lose shape and texture if cooked for too long. Once again, do check the package instructions carefully for perfect results.

The wonderful aroma of the flavorings used in Thai soups is enough to make your mouth water. Once you have found the flavors you like best, you can start experimenting yourself. Some of the soups here are so thin that the stock is transparent, but others, containing rice and eggs, are really thick and very filling. So have fun and play round with the wonderful Thai flavors that make each soup a treat to eat.

hot-and-sour soup
tom yam

SERVES 4

6 dried shiitake mushrooms

4 oz/115 g rice vermicelli noodles

4 small fresh green chiles, seeded and chopped

6 tbsp rice wine vinegar

3¹/₂ cups vegetable stock

2 lemon grass stalks, snapped in half

4 oz/115 g canned water chestnuts, drained, rinsed, and halved

6 tbsp Thai soy sauce

juice of 1 lime

1 tbsp jaggery or soft, light brown sugar

3 scallions, chopped, to garnish

1 Place the dried mushrooms in a bowl and pour in enough hot water to cover. Set aside to soak for 1 hour. Place the noodles in another bowl and pour in enough hot water to cover. Set aside to soak for 10 minutes. Combine the chiles and rice wine vinegar in a third bowl and set aside.

2 Drain the mushrooms and noodles. Bring the stock to a boil in a large pan. Add the mushrooms, noodles, lemon grass, water chestnuts, soy sauce, lime juice, and sugar, and bring to a boil.

3 Stir in the chile and vinegar mixture and cook for 1–2 minutes. Remove and discard the lemon grass. Ladle the soup into warmed bowls and serve hot, garnished with the scallions.

Any visitor to Thailand will return with vivid impressions of the fabulously carved buildings

shrimp laksa 63
khung

SERVES 4

14 oz/400 g canned coconut milk

1¹/₄ cups vegetable stock

1³/₄ oz/50 g vermicelli rice noodles

1 red bell pepper, seeded and cut into strips

8 oz/225 g canned bamboo shoots, drained and rinsed

2-inch/5-cm piece fresh gingerroot, sliced thinly

3 scallions, chopped

1 tbsp Red Curry Paste (see page 31)

2 tbsp fish sauce

1 tsp jaggery or soft, light brown sugar

6 sprigs fresh Thai basil

12 unshelled cooked shrimp

1 Pour the coconut milk and stock into a pan and bring slowly to a boil. Add the remaining ingredients, except the shrimp, and let simmer gently for 4–5 minutes, until the noodles are cooked.

2 Add the shrimp and let simmer for an additional 1-2 minutes, until heated through. Ladle the soup into small warmed bowls*, dividing the shrimp equally between them, and serve.

*cook's tip

Serve the soup immediately, as the noodles will continue to swell and soak up all the liquid. It tastes so fantastic you won't be able to wait anyway.

Thailand's long coastline means plentiful seafood daily

corn and crab soup
tom jood pu sai khow pod

SERVES 4

2 tbsp vegetable or peanut oil

4 garlic cloves, chopped finely

5 shallots, chopped finely

2 lemon grass stalks, chopped finely

1-inch/2.5-cm piece fresh gingerroot, chopped finely

4 cups chicken stock

14 oz/400 g canned coconut milk

scant 1¹/₂ cups frozen corn kernels

12 oz/350 g canned crabmeat, drained and shredded

2 tbsp fish sauce

juice of 1 lime

1 tsp jaggery or soft, light brown sugar

bunch of fresh cilantro, chopped, to garnish

1 Heat the oil in a large skillet and sauté the garlic, shallots, lemon grass, and ginger over low heat, stirring occasionally, for 2–3 minutes, until softened. Add the stock and coconut milk and bring to a boil. Add the corn, reduce the heat, and let simmer gently for 3–4 minutes.

2 Add the crabmeat, fish sauce, lime juice, and sugar, and let simmer gently for 1 minute. Ladle into warmed bowls, garnish with the chopped cilantro, and serve immediately.

Intricate detailing is a feature of Thai architecture everywhere

clear soup with mushrooms and chicken
tom jood gai sai hed

SERVES 4

¼ cup dried cèpes or other mushrooms

4 cups water

2 tbsp vegetable or peanut oil

4 oz/115 g mushrooms, sliced

2 garlic cloves, chopped coarsely

2-inch/5-cm piece fresh galangal, sliced thinly

2 chicken breast portions (on the bone, skin on)

8 oz/225 g baby cremini or white mushrooms, quartered

juice of ½ lime

sprigs fresh flat-leaf parsley, to garnish

1 Place the dried mushrooms in a small bowl and pour over hot water to cover. Set aside to soak for 20–30 minutes. Drain the mushrooms, reserving the soaking liquid. Cut off and discard the stalks and chop the caps coarsely.

2 Pour the reserved soaking water into a pan with the measured water and bring to a boil. Reduce the heat to a simmer.

3 Meanwhile, heat the oil in a wok and stir-fry the soaked mushrooms, sliced fresh mushrooms, garlic, and galangal for 3–4 minutes. Add to the pan of hot water with the chicken breasts. Let simmer for 10–15 minutes, until the meat comes off the bones easily.

4 Remove the chicken from the pan. Peel off and set aside the skin. Remove the meat from the bones, slice and set aside. Return the skin and bones to the stock and let simmer for an additional 30 minutes.

5 Remove the pan from the heat and strain the stock into a clean pan through a cheesecloth-lined strainer. Bring back to a boil and add the cremini or white mushrooms, sliced chicken, and lime juice. Reduce the heat and let simmer for 8-10 minutes. Ladle into warmed bowls, garnish with parsley sprigs, and serve immediately.

The crisp outline of temples and palaces etches into the night sky

seafood and basil soup 69
tom jood ta-la sai bai hu la pa

SERVES 4

2 tbsp vegetable or peanut oil

4 shallots, chopped finely

2 garlic cloves, chopped

2 tsp ground turmeric

2 lemon grass stalks, snapped into three pieces

2 fresh green chiles, seeded and sliced

3 cilantro roots, chopped

3 large tomatoes, peeled (see page 24), seeded, and
   chopped, or 14 oz/400 g canned tomatoes, chopped

3¹/₂ cups fish stock

2 tsp jaggery or soft, light brown sugar

2 tbsp fish sauce

8 oz/225 g live mussels

12 uncooked king shrimp, shelled with tails left intact

8 oz/225 g white fish fillet, skinned and cut into
   large cubes

8 oz/225 g squid, cut into rings

juice of 1 lime

3-4 sprigs fresh Thai basil

1 Heat the oil in a wok or large skillet and stir-fry the
shallots, garlic, turmeric, lemon grass, chiles, and
cilantro for 1–2 minutes to release the flavors.

2 Add the chopped tomatoes, stock, sugar, and fish
sauce, and let simmer for 8–10 minutes.

3 Scrub the mussels under cold running water and
tug off the beards. Discard any with broken or
damaged shells and those that do not shut immediately
when sharply tapped.

4 Add the shrimp, mussels, the white fish cubes, and
squid to the wok or skillet, cover, and let simmer
for 3–5 minutes, until the fish is cooked and the
mussels have opened. Discard any mussels that remain
closed. Stir in the lime juice and Thai basil leaves, ladle
into warmed bowls, and serve immediately.

Left *Auspicious symbols are much in evidence in
Thai carving and sculpture*

Overleaf *Fiery hot chiles are to be handled with care*

rice noodles with tofu soup
guay tiaw tao hu

SERVES 4

7 oz/200 g firm tofu, drained

vegetable or peanut oil, for deep-frying

4 cups vegetable stock

5 scallions, halved

1 yellow bell pepper, seeded and sliced

2 celery stalks, sliced

1 small onion, sliced thinly

4 kaffir lime leaves

2 tbsp Thai soy sauce

1 tbsp Green Curry Paste (see page 31)

6 oz/175 g wide rice noodles, soaked and drained

chopped fresh cilantro, to garnish

Deep-frying tofu before using it for cooking makes it much tastier and more palatable.

1 Using a sharp knife, cut the tofu into even cubes. Pour the oil into a wok to a depth of about 2 inches/5 cm and heat. Deep-fry the tofu, in batches, until browned all over. Remove with a slotted spoon, drain on paper towels, and set aside.

2 Pour the stock into a pan and bring to a boil. Add the scallions, yellow bell pepper, celery, onion, lime leaves, soy sauce, and curry paste, and let simmer for 4–5 minutes. Add the noodles and the tofu and let simmer for 2–3 minutes. Ladle into warmed bowls and serve hot topped with chopped cilantro.

duck with scallion soup
ped kub ton hom

SERVES 4

2 duck breasts, skin on

2 tbsp Red Curry Paste (see page 31)

2 tbsp vegetable or peanut oil

bunch of scallions, chopped

2 garlic cloves, crushed

2-inch/5-cm piece fresh gingerroot, grated

2 carrots, sliced thinly

1 red bell pepper, seeded and cut into strips

4 cups chicken stock

2 tbsp sweet chili sauce

3-4 tbsp Thai soy sauce

14 oz/400 g canned straw mushrooms, drained

1 Slash the skin of the duck 3 or 4 times with a sharp knife and rub in the curry paste. Cook the duck breasts, skin-side down, in a wok or skillet over high heat for 2–3 minutes. Turn over, reduce the heat, and cook for an additional 3–4 minutes, until cooked through. Lift out and slice thickly. Set aside and keep warm.

2 Meanwhile, heat the oil in a wok or large skillet and stir-fry half the scallions, the garlic, ginger, carrots, and red bell pepper for 2–3 minutes. Pour in the stock and add the chili sauce, soy sauce, and mushrooms. Bring to a boil, reduce the heat, and let simmer for 4–5 minutes.

3 Ladle the soup into warmed bowls, top with the duck slices, and garnish with the remaining scallions. Serve immediately.

pork with rice and egg soup
khao phat mu sai khai

This is a very thick and filling soup. Stir in the chiles and scallions at the last moment so they just soften rather than cook. Remember that as the chiles are almost raw they will be hot.

SERVES 4

12 oz/350 g pork loin, skin on

2 tsp chili paste*

scant ¹/₂ cup jasmine rice

3¹/₂ cups chicken stock

1 tbsp Red Curry Paste (see page 31)

1 tsp shrimp paste

2 lemon grass stalks, snapped in half

2-inch/5-cm piece fresh gingerroot, sliced thinly

2 eggs

4 scallions, chopped

2 fresh red chiles, sliced

4 sprigs fresh Thai basil

1 Preheat the oven to 400°F/200°C. Cut the skin away from the meat and peel back. Spread with chili paste, then fold the skin back over the meat. Place in a roasting pan and roast for 40–45 minutes, until crisp and browned. Slice the meat thickly and then cut into thin strips. Chop the crackling. Set aside.

2 Meanwhile, rinse the rice in cold water several times until the water remains clear. Drain well.

3 Pour the stock into a pan, add the curry paste, shrimp paste, lemon grass, and ginger, and bring to a boil. Add the rice and bring back to a boil. Reduce the heat and let simmer for 10–12 minutes.

4 Break the eggs into the soup and once they start to set, break the yolks and stir through the rice. Let simmer for an additional 3–4 minutes, until the rice is cooked. Stir in the scallions and chiles. Ladle into warmed bowls and serve topped with the hot sliced pork and pieces of crackling. Garnish with the basil sprigs.

*cook's tip
You will find ready-made chili paste in Asian food stores and in larger supermarkets.

spicy beef and noodle soup
guay tiaw tom yam nuea

Thailand's temples and monuments are rich in color and eye-catching detail

SERVES 4

4 cups beef stock

$^2/_3$ cup vegetable or peanut oil

3 oz/85 g rice vermicelli noodles

2 shallots, sliced thinly

2 garlic cloves, crushed

1-inch/2.5-cm piece fresh gingerroot, sliced thinly

8-oz/225-g piece fillet steak, cut into thin strips

2 tbsp Green Curry Paste (see page 31)

2 tbsp Thai soy sauce

1 tbsp fish sauce

chopped fresh cilantro, to garnish

1 Pour the stock into a large pan and bring to a boil. Meanwhile, heat the oil in a wok or large skillet. Add a third of the noodles and cook for 10–20 seconds, until they have puffed up. Lift out with tongs, drain on paper towels, and set aside. Discard all but 2 tablespoons of the oil.

2 Add the shallots, garlic, and ginger to the wok or skillet and stir-fry for 1 minute. Add the beef and curry paste and stir-fry for an additional 3–4 minutes, until tender.

3 Add the beef mixture, the uncooked noodles, soy sauce, and fish sauce to the pan of stock and let simmer for 2–3 minutes, until the noodles have swelled. Serve hot garnished with the chopped cilantro and the reserved crispy noodles.

vegetable and noodle soup
guay tiaw nam sai puk

SERVES 4

2 tbsp vegetable or peanut oil

1 onion, sliced

2 garlic cloves, chopped finely

1 large carrot, cut into thin sticks

1 zucchini, cut into thin sticks

4 oz/115 g broccoli, cut into florets

4 cups vegetable stock

1³/₄ cups coconut milk

3–4 tbsp Thai soy sauce

2 tbsp Red Curry Paste (see page 31)

2 oz/55 g wide rice noodles

³/₄ cup mung or soy bean sprouts

4 tbsp chopped fresh cilantro

1 Heat the oil in a wok or large skillet and stir-fry the onion and garlic for 2–3 minutes. Add the carrot, zucchini, and broccoli and stir-fry for 3–4 minutes, until just tender.

2 Pour in the stock and coconut milk and bring to a boil. Add the soy sauce, curry paste, and noodles, and let simmer for 2–3 minutes, until the noodles have swelled. Stir in the bean sprouts and cilantro and serve immediately.

The carving tradition can be traced back many centuries in Thailand

VEGETARIAN
DISHES

It's not hard to find Thai dishes for vegetarians, since the overwhelming majority of Thai people (over 90 percent) are Buddhists, and so don't eat meat anyway. Meat is not a major part of the Thai diet and even in dishes that do contain it only a very little is used, as it is expensive and is often bulked out with rice, noodles, or vegetables.

There is an amazingly extensive array of vegetables grown in Thailand, ranging from the familiar eggplant and scallion to the more exotic bean sprouts, mung beans, and bitter melon, and an assortment of greens, such as bok choy, Napa cabbage, yard-long beans, and fine beans. These ingredients are not always tasty in their own right, but once mixed together and tossed with some curry paste, they take on a whole new life and complement one another extremely well.

You can make dishes interesting by using a variety of textures as well as flavors. Most vegetarian food can be eaten with just a fork—it puts up no fight when it is eaten. That said, it is important to make sure the diner doesn't get a bowl of soggy, over-cooked and tasteless vegetables. Cooking them quickly helps to retain some crunch, keep their color, and make them interesting to eat as each one picks up a different flavor from the cooking. Marinating some ingredients, stir-frying others, and adding the remaining few at the last minute, or steaming them, contribute different textures and tastes to each meal. When assembled in the serving dish, they look and taste fantastic.

Tofu

Using tofu to provide the protein part of the meal adds a further dimension to the vegetarian meal. This versatile ingredient can be used as it is, but it tastes so much better when deep-fried first. It becomes rather like a firm omelet that is a little chewy and not at all soggy. Cut tofu into cubes and cook, in batches, in hot oil before draining on paper towels. It can be marinated first or can simply be added to the dish once the vegetables are cooked.

Like tofu, nuts are another useful source of protein for vegetarians, adding texture and a pleasing crunch to vegetable dishes. Try, for instance, the Sweet-and-Sour Vegetables with Cashews (see page 88), or Broccoli with Peanuts (see page 103). Nuts, too, are much tastier if they are dry-fried or broiled first, as the oil released from them increases their flavor. Watch carefully, though, as they will burn as soon as you take your eye off them.

The other plentiful ingredients in the vegetarian repertoire are rice and noodles, which of course form a significant part of the Thai diet for meat-eaters too. There are many varieties of noodles (see pages 170–71) and they all cook differently, but basically they just need soaking and are ready to eat quickly. Rice takes longer to cook, but is essential to soak up all the sauces from the curries and other dishes.

Then there are the skins—won ton and egg roll skins—that are used to enclose small packages of food, which are steamed or fried. These require only small amounts of food as a filling and are often used as appetizers, but the larger egg roll skins can be used to make more substantial packages of any tasty mixture. However, the filling does need to be quite dry, as too much liquid will seep out of the roll and make the oil spit and splutter during cooking.

All these different ingredients mean that it is easy to cook a fabulous vegetarian meal and not even notice the meat is missing. So you will be able to impress your vegetarian friends next time they visit. They will be thinking about eating soggy quiche again and instead you will present them with an amazing Thai feast.

Marinating some ingredients, stir-frying others...or steaming them, contribute different textures

vegetable packages
puk hao

If you cannot find the small egg roll skins, buy the larger ones and cut them into 4-inch/ 10-cm squares.

SERVES 4

2 tbsp vegetable or peanut oil

8 oz/225 g potatoes, diced and boiled for 5 minutes

2 garlic cloves, crushed

1 onion, chopped

2 tbsp Green Curry Paste (see page 31)

scant ¹/₂ cup frozen peas, thawed

juice of 1 lime

¹/₂ tsp salt

16 x 4-inch/10-cm square egg roll skins

1 egg, beaten

vegetable or peanut oil, for deep-frying

sweet chili sauce or Thai soy sauce, to serve

1 Heat the oil in a wok or skillet and stir-fry the potatoes, garlic, onion, and curry paste until lightly browned. Stir in the peas, lime juice, and salt, and stir-fry for 1–2 minutes. Remove from the heat.

2 Brush 1 egg roll skin with egg. Put a small spoonful of the potato mixture in the center and fold up the edges to enclose the filling and make a purse-shaped package. Press the skin tightly together to seal the package. Repeat with the remaining skins and filling to make 16 small packages.

3 Heat the oil for deep-frying in a wok. Add the vegetable packages, in batches, and deep-fry for 3–4 minutes, until golden brown. Drain on paper towels and keep warm while you cook the remaining packages. Serve hot with a bowl of chili sauce or soy sauce for dipping.

stuffed eggplants
makuea yad sai

SERVES 4

8 small eggplants*

2 tbsp vegetable or peanut oil

4 shallots, chopped finely

2 garlic cloves, crushed

2 fresh red chiles, seeded and chopped

1 zucchini, chopped coarsely

4 oz/115 g block creamed coconut, chopped

few Thai basil leaves, chopped

small handful of fresh cilantro, chopped

4 tbsp Thai soy sauce

to serve

rice with chopped scallions

sweet chili sauce

1 Preheat the oven to 400°F/200°C. Put the eggplants in a roasting pan and cook for 8–10 minutes, until just softened. Cut in half and scoop out the flesh, reserving the shells.

2 Heat the oil in a wok or large skillet and sauté the shallots, garlic, and chile for 2–3 minutes before adding the zucchinis and eggplant flesh. Add the creamed coconut, the herbs, and soy sauce, and let simmer for 3–4 minutes.

3 Divide the mixture between the eggplant shells. Return to the oven for 5–10 minutes, until hot and serve immediately with rice and sweet chili sauce.

cook's tip
If you can only find large eggplants, one half per person would probably be enough.

sweet-and-sour vegetables with cashews
preow wan puk sai tua ob

SERVES 4

1 tbsp vegetable or peanut oil

1 tsp chili oil

2 onions, sliced

2 carrots, sliced thinly

2 zucchinis, sliced thinly

4 oz/115 g broccoli, cut into florets

4 oz/115 g white mushrooms, sliced

4 oz/115 g small bok choy, halved

2 tbsp jaggery or soft, light brown sugar

2 tbsp Thai soy sauce

1 tbsp rice vinegar

scant 1/2 cup cashews

1 Heat both the oils in a wok or skillet and stir-fry the onions for 1–2 minutes, until they start to soften.

2 Add the carrots, zucchinis, and broccoli, and stir-fry for 2–3 minutes. Add the mushrooms, bok choy, sugar, soy sauce, and rice vinegar, and stir-fry for 1-2 minutes.

3 Meanwhile, dry-fry or toast the cashews. Sprinkle the cashews over the stir-fry and serve immediately.

SERVES 4

2 tbsp vegetable or peanut oil

6 scallions, sliced

1 tbsp Green Curry Paste (see page 31)

4 oz/115 g shiitake mushrooms, halved

4 oz/115 g oyster mushrooms

4 oz/115 g white mushrooms

4 oz/115 g portobello mushrooms, sliced

2 tbsp Thai soy sauce

1 tsp jaggery or soft, light brown sugar

8 oz/225 g canned water chestnuts, drained, rinsed
   and sliced

³/₈ cup bean sprouts

cooked noodles, to serve

mixed mushroom stir-fry
pud hed ruem

1 Heat the oil in a wok or skillet and stir-fry the scallions for 30 seconds. Add the curry paste and stir-fry for 1–2 minutes. Add all the mushrooms and stir-fry over high heat until they are tender.

2 Add the soy sauce, sugar, water chestnuts, and bean sprouts and cook for 1–2 minutes, until heated through and just tender. Serve hot with noodles.

eggplant and bean curry
kaeng ped ma khure sai tua

Look for the pea eggplants that are very popular in Thai cooking, but if you cannot find them, just use the more familiar purple ones.

SERVES 4

2 tbsp vegetable or peanut oil

1 onion, chopped

2 garlic cloves, crushed

2 fresh red chiles, seeded and chopped

1 tbsp Red Curry Paste (see page 31)

1 large eggplant, cut into chunks

4 oz/115 g pea or small eggplants

generous 1 cup baby fava beans

4 oz/115 g fine green beans

1¼ cups vegetable stock

2 oz/55 g block creamed coconut, chopped

3 tbsp Thai soy sauce

1 tsp jaggery or soft, light brown sugar

3 kaffir lime leaves, torn coarsely

4 tbsp chopped fresh cilantro

1 Heat the oil in a wok or large skillet and sauté the onion, garlic, and chiles for 1–2 minutes. Stir in the curry paste and cook for 1–2 minutes.

2 Add the eggplants and cook for 3–4 minutes, until starting to soften. (You may need to add a little more oil as eggplants soak it up quickly.) Add all the beans and stir-fry for 2 minutes.

3 Pour in the stock and add the creamed coconut, soy sauce, sugar, and lime leaves. Bring gently to a boil and cook until the coconut has dissolved. Stir in the cilantro and serve hot.

carrot and pumpkin curry
kaeng ped carrot kub phuk

When pumpkins are not available, use butternut squash instead. Peel, remove the seeds, and cut into cubes before cooking.

SERVES 4

²/₃ cup vegetable stock

1-inch/2.5-cm piece fresh galangal, sliced

2 garlic cloves, chopped

1 lemon grass stalk (white part only), chopped finely

2 fresh red chiles, seeded and chopped

4 carrots, peeled and cut into chunks

8 oz/225 g pumpkin, peeled, seeded, and cut
   into cubes

2 tbsp vegetable or peanut oil

2 shallots, chopped finely

3 tbsp Yellow Curry Paste

1³/₄ cups coconut milk

4–6 sprigs fresh Thai basil

¹/₈ cup toasted pumpkin seeds, to garnish

for the Yellow Curry Paste

3 small fresh orange or yellow chiles, chopped coarsely

3 large garlic cloves, chopped coarsely

4 shallots, chopped coarsely

3 tsp ground turmeric

1 tsp salt

12–15 black peppercorns

1 lemon grass stalk (white part only), chopped coarsely

1-inch/2.5-cm piece fresh gingerroot, chopped

1 Pour the stock into a large pan and bring to a boil. Add the galangal, half the garlic, the lemon grass, and chiles, and let simmer for 5 minutes. Add the carrots and pumpkin and let simmer for 5–6 minutes, until tender.

2 To make the curry paste*, put all the ingredients into a food processor or blender and process to a thick paste, scraping down the sides occasionally and making sure they are well combined.

3 Meanwhile, heat the oil in a wok or skillet and stir-fry the shallots and the remaining garlic for 2–3 minutes. Add the curry paste and stir-fry for 1–2 minutes.

4 Stir the shallot mixture into the pan and add the coconut milk and basil. Let simmer for 2–3 minutes. Serve hot, sprinkled with the toasted pumpkin seeds.

*cook's tip
The Yellow Curry Paste can be stored in the refrigerator and used when required. It will keep for up to 3 weeks. Alternatively, you could fill the spaces in an ice cube tray and freeze—use a cube at a time after thawing for about 30 minutes beforehand.

*Overleaf Statues representing Buddha are built
on a breathtaking scale*

onion, potato, and red bell pepper curry
kaeng ped mun fa rung sai hom yai, phrik yhuak

1 Heat the oil in a wok or large skillet and stir-fry the onions, garlic, ginger, and chile for 2–3 minutes. Add the curry paste and stir-fry over low heat for 2–3 minutes.

2 Add the potatoes, bell peppers, stock, and salt, and cook for 3–4 minutes, until all the vegetables are tender. Stir in the cilantro and serve immediately.

SERVES 4

2 tbsp vegetable or peanut oil

2 red onions, sliced

2 garlic cloves, chopped finely

2-inch/5-cm piece fresh gingerroot, chopped finely

1 fresh red chile, seeded and chopped

1 tbsp Red Curry Paste (see page 31)

8 oz/225 g potatoes, cut into cubes, boiled for 5 minutes, and drained

2 red bell peppers, seeded and diced

1¼ cups vegetable stock

1 tsp salt

4 tbsp chopped fresh cilantro

mixed greens curry
kaeng khiao wan ruam

SERVES 4

2 tbsp vegetable or peanut oil

1 fresh green chile, seeded and chopped

6 scallions, sliced

3 tbsp Green Curry Paste (see page 31)

4 oz/115 g bok choy

4 oz/115 g Napa cabbage

³/₄ cup spinach

4 oz/115 g asparagus

3 celery stalks, sliced diagonally

3 tbsp Thai soy sauce

1 tsp jaggery or soft, light brown sugar

juice of 1 lime

boiled jasmine rice, to serve

1 Heat the oil in a wok or large skillet and stir-fry the chile and scallions for 1–2 minutes. Add the curry paste and stir-fry for 2–3 minutes.

2 Add the bok choy, Napa cabbage, spinach, asparagus, and celery and stir-fry for 3–4 minutes, until just tender.

3 Add the soy sauce, sugar, and lime juice, and cook for 30 seconds to heat through. Serve immediately with boiled jasmine rice.

tofu and green vegetable curry
kaeng khiao wan tao hu

SERVES 4

vegetable or peanut oil, for deep-frying

8 oz/225 g firm tofu, drained and cut into cubes

2 tbsp vegetable or peanut oil

1 tbsp chili oil

2 fresh green chiles, seeded and sliced

2 garlic cloves, crushed

6 scallions, sliced

2 medium zucchinis, cut into sticks

1/2 cucumber, peeled, seeded, and sliced

1 green bell pepper, seeded and sliced

1 small head broccoli, cut into florets

2 oz/55 g fine green beans, halved

scant 1/2 cup frozen peas, thawed

1 1/4 cups vegetable stock

2 oz/55 g block creamed coconut, chopped

2 tbsp Thai soy sauce

1 tsp jaggery or soft, light brown sugar

4 tbsp chopped fresh parsley, to garnish

1 Heat the oil for deep-frying in a skillet and carefully lower in the tofu cubes, in batches, and cook for 2–3 minutes, until golden brown. Remove with a slotted spoon and drain on paper towels.

2 Heat the other oils in a wok and stir-fry the chiles, garlic, and scallions for 2–3 minutes. Add the zucchinis, cucumber, green bell pepper, broccoli, and green beans, and stir-fry for an additional 2–3 minutes.

3 Add the peas, stock, coconut, soy sauce, and sugar. Cover and let simmer for 2–3 minutes, until all the vegetables are tender and the coconut has dissolved.

4 Stir in the tofu and serve immediately, sprinkled with the parsley.

zucchini and cashew curry
kaeng courgette med mamuang

SERVES 4

2 tbsp vegetable or peanut oil

6 scallions, chopped

2 garlic cloves, chopped

2 fresh green chiles, seeded and chopped

1 lb/450 g zucchinis, cut into thick slices*

4 oz/115 g shiitake mushrooms, halved

³/₈ cup bean sprouts

¹/₂ cup cashews, toasted or dry-fried

few Chinese chives, chopped

4 tbsp Thai soy sauce

1 tsp fish sauce

rice or noodles, to serve

1 Heat the oil in a wok or large skillet and sauté the onions, garlic, and chiles for 1–2 minutes, until softened but not browned.

2 Add the zucchinis and mushrooms and cook for 2–3 minutes until tender.

3 Add the bean sprouts, nuts, chives, and both sauces and stir-fry for 1–2 minutes.

4 Serve hot with rice or noodles.

*cook's tip
Try to find small zucchinis. Slices of larger ones might need to be cut in half before cooking.

broccoli with peanuts

pud thai broccoli sai tua ob

SERVES 4

3 tbsp vegetable or peanut oil

1 lemon grass stalk, chopped coarsely

2 fresh red chiles, seeded and chopped

1-inch/2.5-cm piece fresh gingerroot, grated

3 kaffir lime leaves, torn coarsely

3 tbsp Green Curry Paste (see page 31)

1 onion, chopped

1 red bell pepper, seeded and chopped

12 oz/350 g broccoli, cut into florets

4 oz/115 g fine green beans

scant ¹/₂ cup unsalted peanuts

1 Put 2 tablespoons of the oil, the lemon grass, chiles, ginger, lime leaves, and curry paste into a food processor or blender and process to a paste.

2 Heat the remaining oil in a wok, add the spice paste, onion, and bell pepper and stir-fry for 2–3 minutes, until the vegetables start to soften.

3 Add the broccoli and green beans, cover and cook over low heat, stirring occasionally, for 4–5 minutes, until tender.

4 Meanwhile, toast or dry-fry the peanuts until lightly browned. Add them to the broccoli mixture and toss together. Serve immediately.

Vivid color is everywhere in the streets— and on the waterways—of Thailand

vegetables with tofu and spinach
pud puk sai tao hu

1 Heat the oil in a skillet and deep-fry the tofu cubes, in batches, for 4–5 minutes, until crisp and browned. Remove with a slotted spoon and drain on paper towels.

2 Heat 2 tablespoons of the oil in a wok or skillet and stir-fry the onions, garlic, and chile for 1–2 minutes, until they start to soften. Add the celery, mushrooms, corn, and red bell pepper, and stir-fry for 3–4 minutes, until they soften.

3 Stir in the curry paste and coconut milk and gradually bring to a boil. Add the sugar and soy sauce and then the spinach. Cook, stirring constantly, until the spinach has wilted. Serve immediately, topped with the tofu.

SERVES 4

vegetable or peanut oil, for deep-frying

8 oz/225 g firm tofu, drained and cut into cubes

2 tbsp vegetable or peanut oil

2 onions, chopped

2 garlic cloves, chopped

1 fresh red chile, seeded and sliced

3 celery stalks, sliced diagonally

8 oz/225 g mushrooms, sliced thickly

4 oz/115 g baby corn, cut in half

1 red bell pepper, seeded and cut into strips

3 tbsp Red Curry Paste (see page 31)

1³/₄ cups coconut milk

1 tsp jaggery or soft, light brown sugar

2 tbsp Thai soy sauce

5 cups baby spinach leaves

Shrine at the Grand Palace in Bangkok. Visitors are expected to dress and behave with respect when visiting shrines and temples

MAIN MEALS

Just as appetizers are not part of Thai culinary culture, the Thai people don't have main courses either, simply because they usually serve all their dishes together and eat them at the same time, making meals very sociable occasions. When I selected the recipes in this chapter I had in mind the way many people in the West organize their meals.

A lot of us eat breakfast, a light snack at lunchtime and have the main meal in the evening—precisely when everyone comes home exhausted.

Part of the attraction of Thai food is the speed with which it is cooked and the fact that some of the preparation can be done in advance. Ideal for weary workers who still want to eat a delicious meal! Meat can be cut up and left in a marinade, onions and garlic can be peeled and bagged, vegetables trimmed, cut to size and left in a bag or box. Rice and noodles can be weighed, ready to prepare on your return. Once you are home, the meal can be cooked in next

Meals in Thailand will usually include an assortment of salads, but these are given their own chapter (see page 196–231). I think we tend to like a hot meal when we come home in the evening and in this chapter we concentrate on hot dishes. However, a lot of the dishes you'll find in this section can be cooked and served cold or eaten cold the following day.

Most of these recipes would be served with rice or noodles to soak up sauces and to add a modifying flavor to the spicier dishes so that there is a mixture of hot and cooler tastes. (Of course we all have differing appetites and spice tolerance-levels so adjust the amounts to suit your family or guests.)

The seasonings used in Thai food mean that by its very nature it will be hot, spicy and tasty. There are lots of curries—not blow-your-brains out... but delicate, tongue-tingling ones

to no time, so you will spend as little time in the kitchen as possible. For those who like to cook, there is great pleasure and relaxation to be had from preparing food, so there is something for everyone in this style of cooking—quick and easy meals for some; fish to skin and cube, shrimp to shell, and curry pastes to make for others.

The seasonings used in Thai food mean that by its very nature it will be hot, spicy, and tasty. There are lots of curries—not blow-your-brains-out Indian vindaloos, but delicate, tongue-tingling ones that affect every area of your mouth. As well as these types of recipe, I have included other traditional and recognizable dishes—but with a Thai twist.

Chili sauce or soy sauce can be served separately with meals so people can use them as condiments or as dips if they like.

What do you drink with Thai food? I would suggest jasmine tea, Singha beer, fruit juice, or a fruity white wine. Remember: if you find the food hot, wait until you've finished before you sip a cold drink. Drinking as you eat only makes the spices seem hotter.

It is great fun learning a new skill and style of cooking, as well as finding out about another country and its ways of eating. You will soon become accustomed to the vibrant flavors and be cooking Thai dishes more often. The only trouble will be that your friends will also enjoy your cooking so much, they will be round for dinner every night!

green chicken curry
kaeng khiao wan gai

SERVES 4

1 tbsp vegetable or peanut oil

1 onion, sliced

1 garlic clove, chopped finely

2–3 tbsp Green Curry Paste (see page 31)

1³/₄ cups coconut milk

²/₃ cup chicken stock

4 kaffir lime leaves

4 skinned, boned chicken breasts, cut into cubes

1 tbsp fish sauce

2 tbsp Thai soy sauce

grated rind and juice of ¹/₂ lime

1 tsp jaggery or soft, light brown sugar

4 tbsp chopped fresh cilantro, to garnish

1 Heat the oil in a wok or large skillet and stir-fry the onion and garlic for 1–2 minutes, until starting to soften. Add the curry paste and stir-fry for 1–2 minutes.

2 Add the coconut milk, stock, and lime leaves, bring to a boil and add the chicken. Reduce the heat and let simmer gently for 15–20 minutes, until the chicken is tender.

3 Add the fish sauce, soy sauce, lime rind and juice, and sugar. Cook for 2–3 minutes, until the sugar has dissolved. Serve immediately, garnished with chopped cilantro.

Thailand's tropical climate is ideal for the coconut palm, and the nuts and milk are plentifully used in Thai cuisine

fish in coconut

kaeng ka-ti pla

SERVES 4

2 tbsp vegetable or peanut oil

6 scallions, chopped coarsely

1-inch/2.5-cm piece fresh gingerroot, grated

2–3 tbsp Red Curry Paste (see page 31)

1³/₄ cups coconut milk

²/₃ cup fish stock

4 kaffir lime leaves

1 lemon grass stalk, broken in half

12 oz/350 g white fish fillets, skinned and cut
　　into chunks

8 oz/225 g squid rings and tentacles

8 oz/225 g large cooked shelled shrimp

1 tbsp fish sauce

2 tbsp Thai soy sauce

4 tbsp chopped fresh Chinese chives

boiled jasmine rice with chopped fresh cilantro,
　　to serve

*Visual reminders abound of the many battles
Thailand has known throughout its history*

1　Heat the oil in a wok or large skillet and stir-fry the
scallions and ginger for 1–2 minutes. Add the curry
paste and stir-fry for 1–2 minutes.

2　Add the coconut milk, fish stock, lime leaves, and
lemon grass. Bring to a boil, then reduce the heat
and let simmer for 1 minute.

3　Add the fish, squid, and shrimp, and let simmer for
2–3 minutes, until the fish is cooked. Add the fish
and soy sauces and stir in the chives. Serve immediately
with jasmine rice with fresh cilantro stirred through it.

chicken and peanut curry
kaeng ped gai sai tao ob

SERVES 4

for the Penang Curry Paste

8 large dried red chiles

2 tsp shrimp paste

3 shallots, chopped

2-inch/5-cm piece fresh galangal, chopped

8 garlic cloves, chopped

4 tbsp chopped cilantro root

3 lemon grass stalks (white part only), chopped

grated rind of 1 lime

1 tbsp fish sauce

2 tbsp vegetable or peanut oil

1 tsp salt

6 tbsp crunchy peanut butter

1 tbsp vegetable or peanut oil

2 red onions, sliced

2 tbsp Penang Curry Paste

1³/₄ cups coconut milk

²/₃ cup chicken stock

4 kaffir lime leaves, torn coarsely

1 lemon grass stalk, chopped finely

6 skinned, boned chicken thighs, chopped

1 tbsp fish sauce

2 tbsp Thai soy sauce

1 tsp jaggery or soft, light brown sugar

generous ³/₈ cup unsalted peanuts, roasted and chopped, plus extra to garnish

6 oz/175 g fresh pineapple, chopped coarsely

6-inch/15-cm piece cucumber, peeled, seeded, and sliced thickly, plus extra to garnish

1 First make the curry paste. Cut off and discard the chile stalks and place the chiles in a bowl. Cover with hot water and set aside to soak for 30–45 minutes. Wrap the shrimp paste in foil and broil or dry-fry for 2–3 minutes, turning once or twice. Put the chiles and their soaking water into a blender or food processor. Add the shrimp paste, shallots, galangal, garlic, cilantro root, and lemon grass, and process until finely chopped. Add the lime rind, fish sauce, oil, and salt, and process again. Add the peanut butter and process to make a thick paste, scraping down the sides occasionally*.

2 Heat the oil in a wok and stir-fry the onions for 1 minute. Add the curry paste and stir-fry for 1–2 minutes.

3 Pour in the coconut milk and stock. Add the lime leaves and lemon grass and let simmer for 1 minute. Add the chicken and gradually bring to a boil. Let simmer for 8–10 minutes, until the chicken is tender.

4 Stir in the fish sauce, soy sauce, and sugar, and let simmer for 1–2 minutes. Stir in the peanuts, pineapple, and cucumber, and cook for 30 seconds. Serve immediately, sprinkled with extra nuts and cucumber.

cook's tip
The Penang Curry Paste can be refrigerated or frozen in the same way as the Yellow Curry Paste (see page 93).

stuffed omelet packages
kai yud sai

SERVES 4

8 large eggs

4 tbsp water

2 large fresh red chiles, seeded and chopped

$\frac{1}{2}$ tsp salt

1 tbsp vegetable or peanut oil

4 scallions, chopped

2 tbsp Red Curry Paste (see page 31)

2 skinned, boned chicken breasts, cubed

4 oz/115 g shiitake mushrooms, chopped

to garnish

chopped fresh cilantro

chopped fresh Chinese chives

1 Beat the eggs with the water, the chiles, and salt. Pour one-quarter of the mixture into an 8 inch/20 cm skillet and cook over low heat until set. Slide the omelet out onto a plate and make 3 more in the same way.

2 Meanwhile, heat the oil in a wok and stir-fry the scallions with the curry paste for 1–2 minutes. Add the chicken and mushrooms and stir-fry for 3–4 minutes, until cooked through.

3 Divide the chicken mixture equally between the omelets, piling it up in the center. Fold all the sides over the filling to enclose it and make a square package. Place the omelets, seam-side down, in a single layer in a steamer. Cover with a lid and cook over boiling water for 4–5 minutes until hot. Transfer to warmed plates, sprinkle the chopped herbs over the top, and serve immediately.

barbecue chicken
gai yang

SERVES 4

4 cups chicken stock

8 chicken thighs

1 tbsp lime juice

2 garlic cloves, crushed

2 tbsp Thai soy sauce

1 tbsp fish sauce

2 tbsp chili sauce

1 Bring the stock to a boil in a large wok. Add the chicken and let simmer for 8–10 minutes, until cooked. Remove with a slotted spoon and let cool.

2 Put the cold chicken in a shallow dish. Combine the lime juice, garlic, soy sauce, fish sauce, and chili sauce in a bowl and spoon the mixture over the chicken, turning to coat. Cover with plastic wrap and let chill for 2–3 hours.

3 Cook the chicken thighs over hot coals*, turning them frequently and brushing with the marinade, for 8–10 minutes, until browned and crisp. Serve hot or cold.

*cook's tip
You can also cook the chicken under the broiler or on a ridged grill pan. It is important that the meat is cooked all the way through—this is why it is cooked before barbecuing.

pork with bell peppers
pud moo phrik-thai

SERVES 4

1 tbsp vegetable or peanut oil

1 tbsp chili oil

1 lb/450 g pork fillet, sliced thinly

2 tbsp green chili sauce

6 scallions, sliced

1-inch/2.5-cm piece fresh gingerroot, sliced thinly

1 red bell pepper, seeded and sliced

1 yellow bell pepper, seeded and sliced

1 orange bell pepper, seeded and sliced

1 tbsp fish sauce

2 tbsp Thai soy sauce

juice of ½ lime

4 tbsp chopped fresh parsley

cooked flat rice noodles, to serve

1 Heat both the oils in a wok. Add the pork, in batches, and stir-fry until browned all over. Remove with a slotted spoon and set aside.

2 Add the chili sauce, scallions, and ginger to the wok and stir-fry for 1–2 minutes. Add the bell peppers and stir-fry for 2–3 minutes.

3 Return the meat to the wok, stir well, and add the fish sauce, soy sauce, and lime juice. Cook for an additional 1–2 minutes, then stir in the parsley and serve with flat rice noodles.

red curry pork with bell peppers
kaeng moo

SERVES 4

2 tbsp vegetable or peanut oil

1 onion, coarsely chopped

2 garlic cloves, chopped

1 lb/450 g pork fillet, sliced thickly

1 red bell pepper, seeded and cut into squares

6 oz/175 g mushrooms, quartered

2 tbsp Red Curry Paste (see page 31)

4 oz/115 g block creamed coconut, chopped

1¼ cups pork or vegetable stock

2 tbsp Thai soy sauce

4 tomatoes, peeled (see page 24), seeded, and chopped

handful of fresh cilantro, chopped

boiled noodles or rice, to serve

1 Heat the oil in a wok or large skillet and sauté the onion and garlic for 1–2 minutes, until they are softened but not browned.

2 Add the pork slices and stir-fry for 2–3 minutes until browned all over. Add the bell pepper, mushrooms, and curry paste.

3 Dissolve the coconut in the hot stock and add to the wok with the soy sauce. Bring to a boil and let simmer for 4–5 minutes until the liquid has reduced and thickened.

4 Add the tomatoes and cilantro and cook for 1–2 minutes before serving with noodles or rice.

The haunting sound of monastery bells rung by the Buddhist monks is one of the evocative memories of a visit to Thailand

spicy beef with potato
pud ped nuea sai mun fa rung

SERVES 4

1 lb/450 g beef fillet

2 tbsp Thai soy sauce

2 tbsp fish sauce

2 tbsp vegetable or peanut oil

3–4 cilantro roots, chopped

1 tbsp crushed black peppercorns

2 garlic cloves, chopped

1 tbsp jaggery or soft, light brown sugar

12 oz/350 g potatoes, diced

$^2/_3$ cup water

bunch of scallions, chopped

5 cups baby spinach leaves

cooked rice or noodles, to serve

1 Cut the beef into thick slices and place in a shallow dish. Put the soy sauce, fish sauce, 1 tablespoon of the oil, the cilantro roots, peppercorns, garlic, and sugar in a food processor and process to a thick paste. Scrape the paste into the dish and toss the beef to coat. Cover with plastic wrap and set aside to marinate in the refrigerator for at least 3 hours, preferably overnight.

2 Heat the remaining oil in a wok. Lift the beef out of the marinade, reserving the marinade, and cook for 3–4 minutes on each side, until browned. Add the reserved marinade and the potatoes with the measured water and gradually bring to a boil. Let simmer for 6–8 minutes, or until the potatoes are tender.

3 Add the scallions and spinach. Cook gently until the greens have wilted. Serve immediately with rice or noodles.

Intricately adorned dragons are a typical theme in Thai art

coconut beef curry
kaeng ped ka-ti nuea

SERVES 4

for the Mussaman Curry Paste

4 large dried red chiles

2 tsp shrimp paste

3 shallots, chopped finely

3 garlic cloves, chopped finely

1-inch/2.5-cm piece fresh galangal, chopped finely

2 lemon grass stalks (white part only), chopped finely

2 cloves

1 tbsp coriander seeds

1 tbsp cumin seeds

seeds from 3 cardamom pods

1 tsp black peppercorns

1 tsp salt

1 tbsp ground coriander

1 tbsp ground cumin

3 tbsp Mussaman Curry Paste

$^2/_3$ cup water

$2^3/_4$ oz/75 g block creamed coconut

1 lb/450 g beef fillet, cut into strips

$1^3/_4$ cups coconut milk

generous $^3/_8$ cup unsalted peanuts, chopped finely

2 tbsp fish sauce

1 tsp jaggery or soft, light brown sugar

4 kaffir lime leaves

boiled rice with chopped fresh cilantro, to serve

1 First make the curry paste*. Cut off and discard the chile stalks and place the chiles in a bowl. Cover with hot water and set aside to soak for 30–45 minutes. Wrap the shrimp paste in foil and broil or dry-fry for 2–3 minutes, turning once or twice. Remove from the broiler or skillet. Dry-fry the shallots, garlic, galangal, lemon grass, cloves, coriander, cumin, and cardamom seeds over low heat, stirring frequently, for 3–4 minutes, until lightly browned. Transfer to a food processor and process until finely ground. Add the chiles and their soaking water, peppercorns, and salt, and process again. Add the shrimp paste and process again to a smooth paste, scraping down the sides as necessary.

2 Combine the coriander, cumin, and curry paste in a bowl. Pour the measured water into a pan, add the creamed coconut and heat until it has dissolved. Add the curry paste mixture and let simmer for 1 minute.

3 Add the beef and let simmer for 6–8 minutes, then add the coconut milk, peanuts, fish sauce, and sugar. Let simmer gently for 15–20 minutes, until the meat is tender.

4 Add the lime leaves and let simmer for 1–2 minutes. Serve the curry hot with rice with freshly chopped cilantro stirred through it.

*cook's tip

The Mussaman Curry Paste can be refrigerated or frozen in the same way as the Yellow Curry Paste (see page 93).

angler fish with lime and chili sauce
yum pla

SERVES 4

4 x 4 oz/115 g angler fish fillets

¹/₄ cup rice flour or cornstarch

6 tbsp vegetable or peanut oil

4 garlic cloves, crushed

2 large fresh red chiles, seeded and sliced

2 tsp jaggery or soft, light brown sugar

juice of 2 limes

grated rind of 1 lime

boiled rice, to serve

1 Toss the fish in the flour, shaking off any excess. Heat the oil in a wok and cook the fish on all sides until browned and cooked through, taking care when turning not to break it up.

2 Lift the fish out of the wok and keep warm. Add the garlic and chiles and stir-fry for 1–2 minutes, until they have softened.

3 Add the sugar, the lime juice and rind, and 2–3 tablespoons of water and bring to a boil. Let simmer gently for 1–2 minutes, then spoon the mixture over the fish. Serve immediately with rice.

Left In contrast to the simple life led by Buddhist monks, temples and shrines are frequently embellished in gold

Overleaf Temple ruins are a common sight in the north of Thailand which in the past was the most easily conquered part of the country

gingered chicken kabobs
kebab gai khing

Thailand's interior includes some spectacular sights that are little known outside the country

SERVES 4

3 skinned, boned chicken breasts, cut into cubes

juice of 1 lime

1-inch/2.5-cm piece gingerroot, peeled and chopped

1 fresh red chile, seeded and sliced

2 tbsp vegetable or peanut oil

1 onion, sliced

2 garlic cloves, chopped

1 eggplant, cut into chunks

2 zucchinis, cut into thick slices

1 red bell pepper, seeded and cut into squares

2 tbsp Red Curry Paste (see page 31)

2 tbsp Thai soy sauce

1 tsp jaggery or soft, light brown sugar

boiled rice, with chopped coriander, to serve

1 Put the chicken cubes in a shallow dish. Mix the lime, ginger, and chile together and pour over the chicken pieces. Stir gently to coat. Cover and let chill for at least 3 hours to marinate.

2 Thread the chicken pieces onto soaked wooden skewers and cook under a hot broiler for 3–4 minutes, turning often, until cooked through.

3 Meanwhile, heat the oil in a wok or large skillet and sauté the onion and garlic for 1–2 minutes, until softened but not browned. Add the eggplant, zucchini, and bell pepper and cook for 3–4 minutes, until cooked but still firm. Add the curry paste, soy sauce, and sugar, and cook for 1 minute.

4 Serve hot with boiled rice, stirred through with chopped coriander.

ground chicken skewers
gai ping

SERVES 4

2 cups ground chicken

1 onion, chopped finely

1 fresh red chile, seeded and chopped

2 tbsp Red Curry Paste (see page 31)

1 tsp jaggery or soft, light brown sugar

1 tsp ground coriander

1 tsp ground cumin

1 egg white

8 lemon grass stalks

boiled rice with chopped scallion, to serve

1 Combine the chicken, onion, chile, curry paste, and sugar in a bowl and stir well to make a thick paste. Stir in the ground coriander, cumin, and egg white, and mix again.

2 Divide the mixture into 8 equal portions and squeeze them round each of the lemon grass stalks. Arrange on a grill pan and cook under high heat, turning frequently, until browned and cooked through. Serve hot with the rice with the scallion stirred through it.

Red and gold are frequently used colors in Thai ornamentation

pork and crab meatballs
mu, pu pan kon thot

SERVES 6

8 oz/225 g pork fillet, chopped finely

5¾ oz/170 g canned crabmeat, drained

3 scallions, chopped finely

1 garlic clove, chopped finely

1 tsp Red Curry Paste (see page 31)

1 tbsp cornstarch

1 egg white

vegetable or peanut oil, for deep-frying

boiled rice, to serve

for the sauce

1 tbsp vegetable or peanut oil

2 shallots, chopped

1 garlic clove, crushed

2 large fresh red chiles, seeded and chopped

4 scallions, chopped

3 tomatoes, chopped coarsely

1 Put the pork and crabmeat into a bowl and mix together. Add the scallions, garlic, curry paste, cornstarch, and egg white, and beat well to make a thick paste. With damp hands shape the mixture into walnut-size balls.

2 Heat the oil in a wok and deep-fry the balls, in batches, for 3–4 minutes, turning frequently, until golden brown and cooked. Drain on paper towels and keep warm.

3 To make the sauce, heat the oil in a wok and stir-fry the shallots and garlic for 1–2 minutes. Add the chiles and scallions and stir-fry for 1–2 minutes, then add the tomatoes. Stir together quickly, then spoon the sauce over the pork and crab balls. Serve immediately with rice.

Parts of rural Thailand are stunning, but most tourists head for the main cities and beaches

crispy pork dumplings
moo krob

SERVES 4

1½ cups ground pork

2 tbsp finely chopped fresh cilantro

1 garlic clove, crushed

1 fresh green chile, seeded and chopped

3 tbsp cornstarch

1 egg white

½ tsp salt

16 won ton skins

1 tbsp water

vegetable or peanut oil, for cooking

chili sauce, to serve

1 Put the pork in a bowl and beat in the cilantro, garlic, chile, 1 tablespoon of the cornstarch, the egg white, and salt. Beat together to a thick, smooth texture. With damp hands shape into 16 equal portions and roll into balls.

2 Put a pork ball in the center of each won ton skin. Make a paste by mixing the remaining cornstarch with 1 tablespoon of water. Brush the edges of the skins with the cornstarch paste and gather them up round the filling to make half into small, sack-like packages, and the rest into triangular shapes.

3 Arrange the dumplings in a single layer (in batches if need be) in the top of a steamer and cook over boiling water for 10–15 minutes, until the meat is cooked through.

4 Heat the oil in a wok or large skillet and carefully drop the packages into it. Deep-fry for 2–3 minutes, until golden brown and crisp. Drain on paper towels and serve hot with chili sauce.

The fabulous gold shrines and temples make a visit to Thailand an unforgettable experience

mussaman curry
kaeng mussaman

SERVES 4

1 tbsp vegetable or peanut oil

1 lb/450 g beef topside, cut into cubes

2 tbsp Mussaman Curry Paste (see page 124)

2 large onions, cut into wedges

2 large potatoes, cut into chunks

1³/₄ cups coconut milk

²/₃ cup water

2 cardamom pods

2 tbsp tamarind paste

2 tsp jaggery or soft, light brown sugar

²/₃ cup unsalted peanuts, toasted or dry-fried

1 fresh red chile, sliced thinly

boiled rice, to serve

1 Heat the oil in a wok and cook the meat, in batches, until browned all over. Remove with a slotted spoon and set aside.

2 Add the curry paste to the wok and stir-fry for 1–2 minutes. Add the onions and potatoes and stir-fry for 4–5 minutes, until golden brown. Remove with a slotted spoon and set aside.

3 Pour the coconut milk into the wok with the measured water and bring to a boil. Reduce the heat and let simmer for 8–10 minutes.

4 Return the meat and cooked vegetables to the wok. Add the cardamoms, tamarind paste, and sugar, and let simmer for 15–20 minutes, until the meat is tender. Stir in the peanuts and chile and serve with rice.

Northern Thailand is where the early Thai kingdoms first developed, and shrines and temples abound

shrimp with noodles
guay tiaw kung

SERVES 4

1 lb/450 g uncooked jumbo shrimp

1 tbsp vegetable or peanut oil

3 shallots, chopped finely

2 garlic cloves, chopped finely

1-inch/2.5-cm piece fresh gingerroot, sliced thinly

1³/₄ cups canned coconut milk

1 tbsp Green Curry Paste (see page 31)

3–4 fresh Thai basil leaves

1 tsp jaggery or soft, light brown sugar

8 oz/225 g flat rice noodles

2 tsp sesame oil

2 tbsp sesame seeds, toasted

sprigs fresh Thai basil, to garnish

1 Remove and discard the heads and shell the shrimp. Cut a slit along the back of each and remove and discard the dark vein.

2 Heat the oil in a wok and stir-fry the shallots, garlic, and ginger for 2–3 minutes. Add the coconut milk and curry paste and let simmer for 2–3 minutes.

3 Add the shrimp, basil leaves, and sugar, and cook until the shrimp turn pink.

4 Meanwhile, cook the noodles in boiling water according to the package instructions, then drain well. Stir in the sesame oil and seeds, garnish with the sprigs of basil, and serve immediately with the shrimp.

Attention to color and detail is evident everywhere in Thailand

fish curry with rice noodles

guay tiaw kaeng pla

SERVES 4

2 tbsp vegetable or peanut oil

1 large onion, chopped

2 garlic cloves, chopped

3 oz/75 g white mushrooms

8 oz/225 g angler fish, cut into cubes,
  each about 1 inch/2.5 cm

8 oz/225 g salmon fillets, cut into cubes,
  each about 1 inch/2.5 cm

8 oz/225 g cod, cut into cubes,
  each about 1 inch/2.5 cm

2 tbsp Red Curry Paste (see page 31)

1³/₄ cups canned coconut milk

handful of fresh cilantro, chopped

1 tsp jaggery or soft, light brown sugar

1 tsp fish sauce

4 oz/115 g rice noodles

3 scallions, chopped

³/₈ cup bean sprouts

few Thai basil leaves

1 Heat the oil in a wok or large skillet and gently sauté the onion, garlic, and mushrooms until softened but not browned.

2 Add the fish, curry paste, and coconut milk and bring gently to a boil. Let simmer for 2–3 minutes before adding half the the cilantro, the sugar, and fish sauce. Keep warm.

3 Meanwhile, soak the noodles for 3–4 minutes (check the package instructions) or until tender and drain well through a colander. Put the colander and noodles over a pan of simmering water. Add the scallions, bean sprouts, and most of the basil and steam on top of the noodles for 1–2 minutes or until just wilted.

4 Pile the noodles onto warmed serving plates and top with the fish curry. Sprinkle the remaining cilantro and basil over the top and serve immediately.

mixed seafood curry
pok tak

SERVES 4

1 tbsp vegetable or peanut oil

3 shallots, chopped finely

1-inch/2.5-cm piece fresh galangal, peeled and

    sliced thinly

2 garlic cloves, chopped finely

1³/₄ cups canned coconut milk

2 lemon grass stalks, snapped in half

4 tbsp fish sauce

2 tbsp chili sauce

8 oz/225 g uncooked jumbo shrimp, shelled

8 oz/225 g baby squid, cleaned and sliced thickly

8 oz/225 g salmon fillet, skinned and cut into chunks

6 oz/175 g tuna steak, cut into chunks

8 oz/225 g fresh mussels, scrubbed and debearded

fresh Chinese chives, to garnish

boiled rice, to serve

1 Heat the oil in a large wok and stir-fry the shallots, galangal, and garlic for 1–2 minutes, until they start to soften. Add the coconut milk, lemon grass, fish sauce, and chili sauce. Bring to a boil, reduce the heat, and let simmer for 1–2 minutes.

2 Add the shrimp, squid, salmon, and tuna, and let simmer for 3–4 minutes, until the shrimp have turned pink and the fish is cooked.

3 Add the mussels and cover with a lid. Let simmer for 1–2 minutes, until they have opened. Discard any mussels that remain closed. Garnish with Chinese chives and serve immediately with rice.

At a temple, hardly any
surface is left unadorned

STIR-FRIED MEALS

The wok is the essential cooking pot used in Far Eastern cooking. It is hugely versatile, comes in several sizes, and is cheap to buy. Woks do need a bit of looking after, but doesn't that apply to any favorite tool in the kitchen? It is much harder to stir-fry in an ordinary skillet, as there is no room to toss the food or push vegetables to one side while you add other ingredients.

Looking at our photographs, you may think the woks look huge, but they need to be big for precisely these reasons—room to toss and stir-fry the food, keeping it moving as it cooks.

Gas is the best fuel for stir-frying, as the flames can lick round the outside of the wok, heating the sides as well as the bottom, but most flat-bottom woks will work on an electric stove. You will need to buy a specialist wok if you cook on a ceramic or an induction stove.

The secret of successful stir-frying is that there is no secret—it's all totally obvious. The wok and oil need to be hot, but not smoking, the meat and vegetables should all be cut to a similar size so they cook in the same time, and the hardest, toughest food should be cooked first, adding the softer, more delicate things at the last moment. The wet sauces and pastes are usually added once the vegetables and meat are almost cooked. So it's easy and fast, ideal for starving students and people in a hurry. Fast, furious, and fun, even the kids can manage it— under supervision.

However, it is essential that you have everything prepared before you start cooking. Choose fresh, crisp young vegetables. Bendy old carrots will not become crunchy during cooking and soggy scallions will always be just that. Peel and chop or slice all the vegetables. It doesn't matter whether you cut them into thin sticks or just slice them, but make sure that

they are all a similar size and that you trim off any ragged ends. It's a good idea to assemble the ingredients in the order in which I list them, because that is the order in which they are cooked.

Meat is usually sliced thinly and then cut into strips. Cut across the grain of beef to break up the tough fibers and to help make it tender. The most popular meat is chicken and this does cook quickly, and it is less fibrous than lamb or beef. It is more economical to buy boned breast portions and to pull off the skin yourself rather than use prepared breasts. Keep an eye open for corn-fed chicken as it has more flavor. As with other meats, it will need to be sliced or cut into cubes.

Have all the sauces and pastes ready to hand so

The secret of successful stir-frying is that there is no secret—it's all totally obvious

there won't be any rushing round at the last minute. Don't hesitate to use ready-made curry pastes to speed things along, but be prepared for the strong smell and slightly stinging eyes when stirring in these prepared spicy additions to the ingredients (the same applies to fresh chiles).

I have given precise measurements for sauces and pastes but if you cook by eye, that's fine. However, remember to taste as you go and keep adjusting the flavors, adding more soy sauce or chili sauce, for example. (You won't need much salt as the soy sauce and spice pastes are quite salty anyway.)

Have any fresh basil or cilantro chopped to add to the wok just before serving so they have time to add flavor, but not disintegrate. So you are all set, now it's just go, go, go...dinner in 10 minutes!

shredded chicken and mixed mushrooms
gai sai hed ruam

SERVES 4

2 tbsp vegetable or peanut oil

2 skinned, boned chicken breasts

1 red onion, sliced

2 garlic cloves, chopped finely

1-inch/2.5-cm piece fresh gingerroot, grated

4 oz/115 g baby white mushrooms

4 oz/115 g shiitake mushrooms, halved

4 oz/115 g cremini mushrooms, sliced

2–3 tbsp Green Curry Paste (see page 31)

2 tbsp Thai soy sauce

4 tbsp chopped fresh parsley

boiled noodles or rice, to serve

1 Heat the oil in a wok and cook the chicken on all sides until lightly browned and cooked through. Remove with a slotted spoon, shred into even-size pieces, and set aside.

2 Pour off any excess oil, then stir-fry the onion, garlic, and ginger for 1–2 minutes, until softened. Add the mushrooms and stir-fry for 2–3 minutes, until they start to brown.

3 Add the curry paste, soy sauce, and shredded chicken to the wok and stir-fry for 1–2 minutes. Stir in the parsley and serve immediately with noodles or rice.

Samtors, *Thailand's 3-wheeler taxis, known as* tuk-tuks, *are one way to get round*

shrimp with scallions and straw mushrooms
kung sai tun-hom la hed

SERVES 4

2 tbsp vegetable or peanut oil

bunch of scallions, chopped

2 garlic cloves, chopped finely

6 oz/175 g block creamed coconut, chopped coarsely

2 tbsp Red Curry Paste (see page 31)

scant 2 cups fish stock

2 tbsp fish sauce

2 tbsp Thai soy sauce

6 sprigs fresh Thai basil

14 oz/400 g canned straw mushrooms, drained

12 oz/350 g large cooked shelled shrimp

boiled jasmine rice, to serve

1 Heat the oil in a wok and stir-fry the scallions and garlic for 2–3 minutes. Add the creamed coconut, red curry paste, and stock, and heat gently until the coconut has dissolved.

2 Stir in the fish sauce and soy sauce, then add the basil, mushrooms, and shrimp. Gradually bring to a boil and serve immediately with jasmine rice.

The carved stone faces of gods and emperors record Thailand's history

cauliflower and beans with cashews
daung-ka-lum sai tau khiao, tao ob

SERVES 4

1 tbsp vegetable or peanut oil

1 tbsp chili oil

1 onion, chopped

2 garlic cloves, chopped

2 tbsp Red Curry Paste (see page 31)

1 small cauliflower, cut into florets

6 oz/175 g yard-long beans, cut into 3-inch/7.5-cm lengths

$^2/_3$ cup vegetable stock

2 tbsp Thai soy sauce

scant $^1/_3$ cup toasted cashews, to garnish

1 Heat both the oils in a wok and stir-fry the onion and garlic until softened. Add the curry paste and stir-fry for 1–2 minutes.

2 Add the cauliflower and beans and stir-fry for 3–4 minutes, until softened. Pour in the stock and soy sauce and let simmer for 1–2 minutes. Serve immediately, garnished with the cashews.

duck with mixed bell peppers
ped kub phrik thai

SERVES 4

1 tbsp vegetable or peanut oil

2 duck breasts, skin on

1 onion, sliced

2 garlic cloves, chopped

1 red bell pepper, seeded and chopped

1 green bell pepper, seeded and chopped

1 yellow bell pepper, seeded and chopped

4 tomatoes, peeled (see page 24), seeded,
   and chopped

²/₃ cup stock

3 tbsp Thai soy sauce

boiled noodles, to serve

1 Heat the oil in a wok and cook the duck breasts over high heat until crisp and brown. Turn over and cook until cooked through. Lift out and keep warm.

2 Pour off any excess fat and stir-fry the onion and garlic for 2–3 minutes, until softened and lightly browned.

3 Add the bell peppers and stir-fry for 2–3 minutes, until tender. Add the tomatoes, stock, and soy sauce, and let simmer for 1–2 minutes. Transfer to a serving plate. Slice the duck thickly and arrange on top, spooning any sauce over it. Serve with noodles.

ginger chicken with noodles
guay tiaw gai sai khing

SERVES 4

2 tbsp vegetable or peanut oil

1 onion, sliced

2 garlic cloves, chopped finely

2-inch/5-cm piece fresh gingerroot, sliced thinly

2 carrots, sliced thinly

4 skinned, boned chicken breasts, cut
  into cubes

1¼ cups chicken stock

4 tbsp Thai soy sauce

8 oz/225 g canned bamboo shoots, drained and rinsed

2¾ oz/75 g flat rice noodles

for the garnish

4 scallions, chopped

4 tbsp chopped fresh cilantro

1 Heat the oil in a wok and stir-fry the onion, garlic, ginger, and carrots for 1–2 minutes, until softened. Add the chicken and stir-fry for 3–4 minutes, until the chicken is cooked through and lightly browned.

2 Add the stock, soy sauce, and bamboo shoots, and gradually bring to a boil. Let simmer for 2–3 minutes. Meanwhile, soak the noodles in boiling water for 6–8 minutes. Drain well. Garnish with the scallions and cilantro and serve immediately, with the chicken stir-fry.

Right *Gifts and flowers are offered up to sacred shrines*

Overleaf *Homes on the rivers of Thailand's central plains are built on stilts*

mixed vegetables with quick-fried basil
pud puk ruam ka-preow tord grob

SERVES 4

2 tbsp vegetable or peanut oil

2 garlic cloves, chopped

1 onion, sliced

4 oz/115 g baby corn, cut in half diagonally

¹/₂ cucumber, peeled, halved, seeded, and sliced

8 oz/225 g canned water chestnuts, drained and rinsed

2 oz/55 g snow peas, trimmed

4 oz/115 g shiitake mushrooms

1 red bell pepper, seeded and sliced thinly

1 tbsp jaggery or soft, light brown sugar

2 tbsp Thai soy sauce

1 tbsp fish sauce

1 tbsp rice vinegar

boiled rice, to serve

for the quick-fried basil

vegetable or peanut oil, for cooking

8-12 sprigs fresh Thai basil

1 Heat the oil in a wok and stir-fry the garlic and onion for 1-2 minutes. Add the corn, cucumber, water chestnuts, snow peas, mushrooms, and red bell pepper, and stir-fry for 2–3 minutes, until starting to soften.

2 Add the sugar, soy sauce, fish sauce, and vinegar, and gradually bring to a boil. Let simmer for 1-2 minutes.

3 Meanwhile, heat the oil for the basil in a wok or skillet and, when hot, add the basil sprigs. Cook for 20–30 seconds, until crisp. Remove with a slotted spoon and drain on paper towels.

4 Garnish the vegetable stir-fry with the crispy basil and serve immediately, with the boiled rice.

chicken with yellow curry sauce
gai pud phung ka-ri

SERVES 4

for the spice paste

6 tbsp Yellow Curry Paste (see page 93)

²/₃ cup plain yogurt

1³/₄ cups water

handful of fresh cilantro, chopped

handful of fresh Thai basil leaves, shredded

for the stir-fry

2 tbsp vegetable or peanut oil

2 onions, cut into thin wedges

2 garlic cloves, chopped finely

2 skinned, boned chicken breasts, cut
  into strips

6 oz/175 g baby corn, halved lengthwise

to garnish

chopped fresh cilantro

shredded fresh basil

1 To make the spice paste, stir-fry the yellow curry
paste in a wok for 2–3 minutes, then stir in the
yogurt, water, and herbs. Bring to a boil, then
let simmer for 2–3 minutes.

2 Meanwhile, heat the oil in a wok and stir-fry the
onions and garlic for 2–3 minutes. Add the chicken
and corn and stir-fry for 3–4 minutes, until the meat
and corn are tender.

3 Stir in the spice paste and bring to a boil. Let
simmer for 2–3 minutes, until heated through.
Serve immediately, garnished with extra herbs if liked.

pork with mixed green beans
pud tua sai mu

1 Heat the oil in a wok and stir-fry the shallots, pork, galangal, and garlic until lightly browned.

2 Add the stock, chili sauce, and peanut butter, and stir until the peanut butter has melted. Add all the beans and let simmer for 3–4 minutes. Serve hot with crispy noodles.

SERVES 4

2 tbsp vegetable or peanut oil

2 shallots, chopped

8 oz/225 g pork fillet, sliced thinly

1-inch/2.5-cm piece fresh galangal, sliced thinly

2 garlic cloves, chopped

1¼ cups chicken stock

4 tbsp chili sauce

4 tbsp crunchy peanut butter

4 oz/115 g fine green beans

generous 1 cup frozen fava beans

4 oz/115 g string beans, sliced

crispy noodles, to serve

beef with onions and broccoli
pud nuea sai hom-yai la thai broccoli

SERVES 4

2 tbsp vegetable or peanut oil

2 tbsp Green Curry Paste (see page 31)

2 x 6 oz/175 g sirloin steaks, sliced thinly

2 onions, sliced

6 scallions, chopped

2 shallots, chopped finely

8 oz/225 g broccoli, cut into florets

1³/₄ cups coconut milk

3 kaffir lime leaves, chopped coarsely

4 tbsp chopped fresh cilantro

few Thai basil leaves

1 Heat the oil in a wok and stir-fry the curry paste for 1–2 minutes. Add the meat, in batches if necessary, and stir-fry until starting to brown.

2 Add the onions, scallions, and shallots, and stir-fry for 2–3 minutes. Add the broccoli and stir-fry for 2–3 minutes.

3 Pour in the coconut milk, add the lime leaves, and bring to a boil. Let simmer gently for 8–10 minutes, until the meat is tender. Stir in the cilantro and basil and serve immediately.

The Asian elephant, a native of Thailand, is an auspicious symbol

squid and red bell peppers

pud pla-muk sai phrik-deang

SERVES 4

for the spice paste

2 tbsp vegetable or peanut oil

1 tbsp chili oil with shrimp

2 shallots, chopped

2–3 large fresh red chiles, seeded and
chopped coarsely

2 tbsp ground coriander

2 tbsp ground cumin

1-inch/2.5-cm piece fresh gingerroot, chopped

1 tbsp finely chopped lemon grass

3–4 cilantro roots, chopped

1 tsp salt

1 tsp jaggery or soft, light brown sugar

for the stir-fry

2 red bell peppers, seeded and diced

$^2/_3$ cup plain yogurt

1 lb 10 oz/750 g squid, cleaned and sliced

juice of 1 lime

4 oz/115 g block creamed coconut, chopped

$^2/_3$ cup hot water

1 Put all the ingredients for the spice paste into a food
processor and process until chopped finely.

2 Scrape the spice paste into a wok and stir-fry
gently for 3–4 minutes. Add the red bell peppers
and stir-fry for 1–2 minutes.

3 Add the yogurt and bring to a boil. Add the
squid and let simmer for 2–3 minutes, then stir in
the lime juice, coconut, and water. Let simmer for an
additional 1–2 minutes, until the coconut dissolves.
Serve immediately.

*Entire meals are cooked in the bottom
of the flat boats that ply the waterways*

NOODLES & RICE

Noodles are probably one of the quickest foods to prepare in the modern world. The larger supermarkets are now full of numerous dried varieties, often ready-flavored, that only need to be covered in boiling water and left for a couple of minutes to swell. Absolutely fabulous for young children and students, noodles are cheap, easy to cook, and taste delicious.

In Thailand it's somewhat different. Noodles are by no means only a quick snack: they're a culinary institution. There are a great many varieties and hundreds of recipes use them as the main ingredient. The type of noodle depends on the flour used to make them—it could be rice flour, mung bean flour, or wheat flour (even though the country does not count wheat among its staple crops)—whereas the name of the noodle depends on the thickness of the strips.

One of the most popular varieties of noodle is the flat, dried rice-flour noodles (*kuay tiaw*), which are widely available, even in supermarkets. Then there are the spaghetti-like fresh rice flour noodles (*kanom jeen*), which are rather like the type used in Malaysia and Singapore. Check out the chiller cabinets in your local supermarket for fresh egg noodles that are quick to cook and are great for adding to soups. Dried wheat-flour noodles are thinner, flatter, and creamier in color than the white dried rice vermicelli (*sen mee*), which are also sometimes known as rice-stick noodles. Dried transparent or jelly noodles (*woon sen*) are used predominantly in soups and salads, rice sticks (*sen lek*) are the thinnest ones available, and the best-known noodles are the thin and wiry rice vermicelli (*kuay tiaw jeen*). These are fun to drop into hot oil and watch puff up. They are rather like shrimp crackers in texture but do not have a lot of taste.

dash of chili oil or with soy sauce poured over them. Or they can be topped with peanuts, as in the popular dish Pad Thai (see page 172), or a few stir-fried vegetables. Because noodles are so quick to prepare and season, street hawkers have traditionally sold them in a variety of ways: soaking them in meat stock, topping them with pieces of stir-fried meat or shrimp, or sprinkling them with sugar or hot red pepper flakes. Pad Thai is traditionally prepared as a dish of stir-fried noodles, cooked quickly in very hot oil in a hot wok, and mixed together with shrimp, beef, eggs, tofu, vegetables, and a variety of seasonings including garlic and scallions. However, it can also make the most stunning vegetarian dish using only the tofu and vegetables.

Noodles taste wonderful as a snack or a meal on their own, with a dash of chili oil or with soy sauce poured over them

Noodles vary in thickness as well. The popular egg noodle (*kuay tiaw–be mee*) is approximately 1/16 inch/2 mm thick, vermicelli are much thinner and the flatter types are obviously wider. All dried noodles can be found in specialist Thai and Chinese food stores, and the larger supermarkets stock an increasing range. The majority can also be found fresh if you seek out the more specialist stores.

Noodles should be soaked or cooked in boiling water, but not for very long. If they are overcooked they will fall apart and become bland and soggy. Some types just need covering with boiling water and leaving for a couple of minutes before draining and using, but do check the package instructions or ask for advice in the food store.

Rather than putting ingredients in with the noodles, as you can when cooking rice, it is more effective to wait until the noodles have been drained before you decide how to flavor them. Noodles taste wonderful as a snack or meal on their own, with a

Along with noodles, rice is the other basic staple food eaten in Thailand, as it is in most countries throughout the Far East—and indeed the Middle East. It is easy and cheap to grow and is produced in vast amounts. Thailand has long been famous for its jasmine rice, which is a popular high-grade variety and, as most of it is exported, it is easily available in the West. This type is often called fragrant or scented rice because of the fabulous smell it produces while it is cooking. Glutinous rice, which is much stickier, can also be used in many sweet recipes. The "stickiness" results from the amount of starch in the rice grains, so if you do want sticky rice, don't rinse off all the starch before cooking: soak it overnight, then steam for 10–15 minutes.

pad thai
phat thai

The best known of all Thai noodle dishes.

SERVES 4

8 oz/225 g thick rice-stick noodles

2 tbsp vegetable or peanut oil

2 garlic cloves, chopped

2 fresh red chiles, seeded and chopped

6 oz/175 g pork fillet, sliced thinly

4 oz/115 g uncooked shrimp, shelled and chopped

8 fresh Chinese chives, chopped

2 tbsp fish sauce

juice of 1 lime

2 tsp jaggery or soft, light brown sugar

2 eggs, beaten

³/₄ cup bean sprouts

4 tbsp chopped fresh cilantro

³/₄ cup unsalted peanuts, chopped, plus extra to serve

crispy fried onions, to serve

1 Soak the noodles in warm water for 10 minutes, drain well, and set aside.

2 Heat the oil in a wok and stir-fry the garlic, chiles, and pork for 2–3 minutes. Add the shrimp and stir-fry for an additional 2–3 minutes.

3 Add the chives and noodles, then cover and cook for 1–2 minutes. Add the fish sauce, lime juice, sugar, and eggs. Cook, stirring and tossing constantly to mix in the eggs.

4 Stir in the bean sprouts, cilantro, and peanuts, and serve with small dishes of crispy fried onions and extra chopped peanuts.

pork with vegetables
pud puk sai moo

SERVES 4

8 tbsp vegetable or peanut oil

4 oz/115 g rice vermicelli noodles

4 belly pork strips, sliced thickly

1 red onion, sliced

2 garlic cloves, chopped

1-inch/2.5-cm piece fresh gingerroot, sliced thinly

1 large fresh red chile, seeded and chopped

4 oz/115 g baby corn, halved lengthwise

1 red bell pepper, seeded and sliced

6 oz/175 g broccoli, cut into florets

5$^{1}/_{2}$ oz/150 g jar black bean sauce

$^{3}/_{4}$ cup bean sprouts

1 Heat the oil in a wok and cook the rice noodles, in batches, for 15–20 seconds, until they puff up. Remove with a slotted spoon, drain on paper towels, and set aside.

2 Pour off all but 2 tablespoons of the oil and stir-fry the pork, onion, garlic, ginger, and chile for 4–5 minutes, or until the meat has browned.

3 Add the corn, red bell pepper, and broccoli and stir-fry for 3–4 minutes, until the vegetables are just tender. Stir in the black bean sauce and bean sprouts, then cook for an additional 2–3 minutes. Serve immediately, topped with the crispy noodles.

stir-fried rice with green vegetables

khao phat puk

SERVES 4

generous 1 cup jasmine rice

2 tbsp vegetable or peanut oil

1 tbsp Green Curry Paste (see page 31)

6 scallions, sliced

2 garlic cloves, crushed

1 zucchini, cut into thin sticks

4 oz/115 g yard-long beans

6 oz/175 g asparagus, trimmed

1 tbsp fish sauce

3–4 fresh Thai basil leaves

1 Cook the rice in lightly salted boiling water for 12–15 minutes, drain well, then cool thoroughly and let chill overnight.

2 Heat the oil in a wok and stir-fry the curry paste for 1 minute. Add the scallions and garlic and stir-fry for 1 minute.

3 Add the zucchini, beans, and asparagus, and stir-fry for 3–4 minutes, until just tender. Break up the rice and add it to the wok. Cook, stirring constantly for 2–3 minutes, until the rice is hot. Stir in the fish sauce and basil leaves. Serve hot.

egg-fried rice with vegetables and crispy onions
khao-khai pak horm-tord

SERVES 4

4 tbsp vegetable or peanut oil

2 garlic cloves, chopped finely

2 fresh red chiles, seeded and chopped

4 oz/115 g mushrooms, sliced

2 oz/55 g snow peas, halved

2 oz/55 g baby corn, halved

3 tbsp Thai soy sauce

1 tbsp jaggery or soft, light brown sugar

few Thai basil leaves

3 cups, cooked and cooled*

2 eggs, beaten

2 onions, sliced

1 Heat half the oil in a wok or large skillet and sauté the garlic and chiles for 2–3 minutes.

2 Add the mushrooms, snow peas, and corn, and stir-fry for 2–3 minutes before adding the soy sauce, sugar, and basil. Stir in the rice.

3 Push the mixture to one side of the wok and add the eggs to the bottom and stir until lightly set before combining into the rice mixture.

4 Heat the remaining oil in another skillet and sauté the onions until crispy and brown. Serve the rice topped with the onions.

cook's tip

The rice must be cold when it is added to the wok, otherwise the egg will combine with it to make a congealed mass.

curried noodles with shrimp and straw mushrooms 179
guay tiaw kung sai hed

SERVES 4

1 tbsp vegetable or peanut oil

3 shallots, chopped

1 fresh red chile, seeded and chopped

1 tbsp Red Curry Paste (see page 31)

1 lemon grass stalk (white part only), chopped finely

8 oz/225 g cooked shelled shrimp

14 oz/400 g canned straw mushrooms, drained

2 tbsp fish sauce

2 tbsp Thai soy sauce

8 oz/225 g fresh egg noodles

fresh cilantro, chopped, to garnish

1 Heat the oil in a wok and stir-fry the shallots and chile for 2–3 minutes. Add the curry paste and lemon grass and stir-fry for 2–3 minutes.

2 Add the shrimp, mushrooms, fish sauce, and soy sauce, and stir well to mix.

3 Meanwhile, cook the noodles in boiling water for 3–4 minutes, drain, and transfer to warmed plates. Top with the shrimp curry, sprinkle the cilantro over, and serve immediately.

The distinctive saffron-colored robes may be seen on statues as well as worn by Buddhist monks

spicy noodles with mushroom egg rolls
guay tiaw tom yam kub po pia hed

SERVES 4

2 tbsp vegetable or peanut oil

1 small onion, chopped finely

8 oz/225 g mushrooms, chopped

1 tbsp Red Curry Paste (see page 31)

1 tbsp Thai soy sauce

1 tbsp fish sauce

8 square egg roll skins

vegetable or peanut oil, for deep-frying

8 oz/225 g quick-cook noodles

1 garlic clove, chopped

6 scallions, chopped

1 red bell pepper, seeded and chopped

1 tbsp ground coriander

1 tbsp ground cumin

1 Heat 1 tablespoon of the oil in a wok and stir-fry the onion and mushrooms until crisp and browned. Add the curry paste, soy sauce, and fish sauce, and stir-fry for 2–3 minutes. Remove the wok from the heat.

2 Spoon an eighth of the mixture across one of the egg roll skins and roll up, folding the sides over the filling to enclose it.

3 Heat the oil for deep-frying in a wok or skillet and deep-fry the egg rolls, 4 at a time, until crisp and browned. Drain on paper towels and keep warm.

4 Meanwhile, put the noodles in a bowl, cover with boiling water, and let swell.

5 Heat the remaining oil in the wok and stir-fry the garlic, scallions, and red bell pepper for 2–3 minutes. Stir in the coriander and cumin, then drain the noodles and add them to the wok. Toss together and serve topped with the egg rolls.

chicken with vegetables and cilantro rice
khao man gai

SERVES 4

2 tbsp vegetable or peanut oil

1 red onion, chopped

2 garlic cloves, chopped

1-inch/2.5-cm piece gingerroot, peeled and chopped

2 skinned, boned chicken breasts, cut into strips

4 oz/115 g white mushrooms

14 oz/400 g canned coconut milk

2 oz/55 g sugar snap peas, trimmed and halved
  lengthwise

2 tbsp soy sauce

1 tbsp fish sauce

for the rice

1 tbsp vegetable or peanut oil

1 red onion, sliced

3 cups rice, cooked and cooled

8 oz/225 g bok choy, torn into large pieces

handful of fresh cilantro, chopped

2 tbsp Thai soy sauce

1 Heat the oil in a wok or large skillet and sauté the onion, garlic, and ginger together for 1–2 minutes.

2 Add the chicken and mushrooms and cook over high heat until browned. Add the coconut milk, sugar snap peas, and sauces, and bring to a boil. Let simmer gently for 4–5 minutes until tender.

3 Heat the oil for the rice in a separate wok or large skillet and cook the onion until softened but not browned. Add the cooked rice, bok choy, and fresh cilantro, and heat gently until the leaves have wilted and the rice is hot. Sprinkle over the soy sauce and serve immediately with the chicken.

Overleaf *Vivid green kaffir limes, and their leaves, provide a key flavoring in Thai cuisine*

shrimp with coconut rice
khao ka-ti khung

SERVES 4

1 cup dried Chinese mushrooms

2 tbsp vegetable or peanut oil

6 scallions, chopped

scant $\frac{1}{2}$ cup dry unsweetened coconut

1 fresh green chile, seeded and chopped

generous 1 cup jasmine rice

$\frac{2}{3}$ cup fish stock

1$\frac{3}{4}$ cups coconut milk

12 oz/350 g cooked shelled shrimp

6 sprigs fresh Thai basil

1 Place the mushrooms in a small bowl, cover with hot water, and set aside to soak for 30 minutes. Drain, then cut off and discard the stalks and slice the caps.

2 Heat 1 tablespoon of the oil in a wok and stir-fry the scallions, coconut, and chile for 2–3 minutes, until lightly browned. Add the mushrooms and stir-fry for 3-4 minutes.

3 Add the rice and stir-fry for 2-3 minutes, then add the stock and bring to a boil. Reduce the heat and add the coconut milk. Let simmer for 10–15 minutes, until the rice is tender. Stir in the shrimp and basil, heat through, and serve.

rice with seafood and squid
khao sai khung la pha-muk

SERVES 4

2 tbsp vegetable or peanut oil

3 shallots, chopped finely

2 garlic cloves, chopped finely

generous 1 cup jasmine rice

1¼ cups fish stock

4 scallions, chopped

2 tbsp Red Curry Paste (see page 31)

8 oz/225 g baby squid, cleaned and sliced thickly

8 oz/225 g white fish fillets, skinned and cut into cubes

8 oz/225 g salmon fillets, skinned and cut into cubes

4 tbsp chopped fresh cilantro

1 Heat 1 tablespoon of the oil in a wok and stir-fry the shallots and garlic for 2–3 minutes, until softened. Add the rice and stir-fry for 2–3 minutes.

2 Add a ladleful of the stock and let simmer, adding more stock as needed, for 12–15 minutes, until tender. Transfer to a dish, let cool, and chill overnight.

3 Heat the remaining oil in a wok and stir-fry the scallions and curry paste for 2–3 minutes. Add the squid and fish and stir-fry gently to avoid breaking up the fish. Stir in the rice and cilantro, heat through gently, and serve.

fish curry
kaeng ped pla

SERVES 4

juice of 1 lime

4 tbsp fish sauce

2 tbsp Thai soy sauce

1 fresh red chile, seeded and chopped

12 oz/350 g angler fish fillet, cut into cubes

12 oz/350 g salmon fillets, skinned and cut into cubes

1³/₄ cups coconut milk

3 kaffir lime leaves

1 tbsp Red Curry Paste (see page 31)

1 lemon grass stalk (white part only), chopped finely

2 cups jasmine rice, boiled

4 tbsp chopped fresh cilantro

1 Combine the lime juice, half the fish sauce, and the soy sauce in a shallow, nonmetallic dish. Add the chile and the fish, stir to coat, cover with plastic wrap, and let chill for 1–2 hours, or overnight.

2 Bring the coconut milk to a boil in a pan and add the lime leaves, curry paste, the remaining fish sauce, and the lemon grass. Let simmer gently for 10–15 minutes.

3 Add the fish and the marinade and let simmer for 4–5 minutes, until the fish is cooked. Serve hot with boiled rice with chopped cilantro stirred through it.

The warm waters of the Andaman Sea are a rich source of seafood

stir-fried rice noodles with marinated fish
guay tiaw pla

SERVES 4

1 lb/450 g angler fish or cod, cubed

8 oz/225 g salmon fillets, cubed

2 tbsp vegetable or peanut oil

2 fresh green chiles, seeded and chopped

grated rind and juice of 1 lime

1 tbsp fish sauce

4 oz/115 g wide rice noodles

2 tbsp vegetable or peanut oil

2 shallots, sliced

2 garlic cloves, chopped finely

1 fresh red chile, seeded and chopped

2 tbsp Thai soy sauce

2 tbsp chili sauce

1 Place the fish in a shallow bowl. To make the marinade, mix the oil, green chiles, lime juice and rind, and fish sauce together and pour over the fish. Cover and let chill for 2 hours.

2 Put the noodles in a bowl and cover with boiling water. Leave for 8–10 minutes (check the package instructions) and drain well.

3 Heat the oil in a wok or large skillet and sauté the shallots, garlic, and red chile until lightly browned. Add the soy sauce and chili sauce. Add the fish and the marinade to the wok and stir-fry gently for 2–3 minutes until cooked through.

4 Add the drained noodles and stir gently. Sprinkle with cilantro and serve immediately.

beef with fresh noodles
guay tiaw nuea

SERVES 4

6 dried black cloud Chinese mushrooms

2 tbsp vegetable or peanut oil

2 x 8 oz/225 g sirloin steaks, sliced thickly

1 onion, cut into thin wedges

2 garlic cloves, chopped

1 green bell pepper, seeded and chopped

3 celery stalks, sliced

2 tbsp Green Curry Paste (see page 31)

1¹/₄ cups beef stock

4 tbsp black bean sauce

8 oz/225 g fresh egg noodles

4 tbsp chopped fresh parsley

1 Put the mushrooms in a bowl, cover with boiling water, and set aside to soak for 30 minutes. Drain. Break up any larger pieces.

2 Heat the oil in a wok and stir-fry the steak over high heat until browned. Add the mushrooms, onion, garlic, bell pepper, and celery, and stir-fry for 3–4 minutes. Add the curry paste, beef stock, and black bean sauce, and stir-fry for 2–3 minutes.

3 Meanwhile, cook the noodles in boiling water for 3–4 minutes, drain well, and stir into the wok. Sprinkle the parsley over and stir. Serve immediately.

The temple of the Emerald Buddha in Bangkok

egg-fried rice with chicken
khao phat gai sai khai

SERVES 4

generous 1 cup jasmine rice

3 skinned, boned chicken breasts, cut into cubes

1³/₄ cups canned coconut milk

1³/₄ oz/50 g block creamed coconut, chopped

2–3 cilantro roots, chopped

thinly pared rind of 1 lemon

1 fresh green chile, seeded and chopped

3 fresh Thai basil leaves

1 tbsp fish sauce

1 tbsp oil

3 eggs, beaten

for the garnish

fresh chives

sprigs fresh cilantro

1 Cook the rice in boiling water for 12–15 minutes, drain well, then let cool, and chill overnight.

2 Put the chicken into a pan and cover with the coconut milk. Add the creamed coconut, cilantro roots, lemon rind, and chile, and bring to a boil. Let simmer for 8–10 minutes, until the chicken is tender. Remove from the heat. Stir in the basil and fish sauce.

3 Meanwhile, heat the oil in a wok and stir-fry the rice for 2–3 minutes. Pour in the eggs and stir until they have cooked and mixed with the rice. Line 4 small ovenproof bowls or ramekins with plastic wrap and pack with the rice. Turn out carefully onto serving plates and remove the plastic wrap. Garnish with long chives and sprigs of cilantro. Serve with the chicken.

*Sculptures and murals adorn
every Thai temple*

SALADS

Often called "yam" dishes, salads accompany most Thai meals and usually consist of a mixture of either raw vegetables or ones that have been cooked quickly, which are served with some crunch still in them. Salads are sometimes served as an appetizer when they are offered just before a meal as something to snack on before the main courses arrive.

That said, as most dishes are usually served almost at the same time at the Thai table, rather than as separate courses, any salads immediately become part of the meal.

Typically, a Thai salad should include hot and intense flavors. These act to stimulate the taste buds ready for the dishes that follow. Chiles, soy and fish sauces, as well as cilantro, garlic, and jaggery all play an important part in many of the salads included here. The combination of these ingredients enhances the meat, fish, or vegetables that are being prepared and cooked, adding that extra dimension of flavor that is quintessentially Thai.

We eat a lot of salads in the West but our traditional dishes are vastly different from the type of salads served in the East. Ours tend to be blander and more leafy, and include only a few ingredients that are tossed in a dressing, whereas Thai salads, like many other Thai dishes, are meant to be spicy and mouth-tingling. This departure from the traditions of our cuisine is in part what makes Thai food such fun to cook and eat. Exposure to different styles of food from round the world has made us much more adventurous in our tastes and cooking skills these days and it's good to experience and experiment with the culinary styles of another culture. Even people who don't relish cooking but like to eat Thai food in restaurants are willing to try new and unusual tastes. But as more food stores stock the exotic and unfamiliar ingredients these days, we can all have a go at tackling Thai food, including salads, at home.

As always, it is vital to use fresh, crispy vegetables because they provide the best flavor and texture, whether they are cooked or eaten raw. Limp or soggy vegetables will produce a soggy salad, so choose the best you can find. Cut everything to a similar size for stir-frying to ensure that they cook evenly and, even if you are serving a cold salad, think about cutting all ingredients into manageable, bite-size pieces so they are easier and a pleasure to eat. Use your biggest wok or skillet to stir-fry the vegetables so there is plenty of room for tossing and enough space to add in noodles or rice if appropriate.

If a recipe includes meat, always cut it into pieces across the grain to make it more tender. Marinating meat adds that extra depth of taste as well as tenderizing it. Keep your pieces the same size so they cook in the same length of time and are still easy to eat. Tofu should also be cut into cubes, and it is best marinated and fried before any final cooking as both processes help to increase the flavor and interest of a fairly bland product.

The recipes here are a real mixture of traditional flavors and contemporary tastes. By no means all of them contain meat because vegetables and fish are cheaper and more popular in Thailand and, of course, the majority of Thai people are vegetarian anyway. But any recipe should be flexible so it's up to you to experiment a little with the flavors and cooking styles. You will find that Thai curry pastes (see page 31), whether bought or homemade, will vary enormously in texture, color, and heat. Some recipes will ask for 2 tablespoons of curry paste, which you may find too hot, so if in doubt add it gradually and keep tasting as you cook. Basically, I would encourage you to cut up lots of fresh and colorful produce and stir-fry it quickly with zesty flavorings to make brilliant and mouthwatering dishes.

Thai salads, like many other Thai dishes, are meant to be spicy and mouth-tingling

duck salad
yum ped

1 Unwrap the duck and let the skin dry out overnight in the refrigerator.

2 The following day, slash the skin side 5 or 6 times. Mix the lemon grass, 2 tablespoons of the vegetable oil, all the sesame oil, fish sauce, chile, and curry paste together in a shallow dish and place the duck breasts in the mixture. Turn to coat and to rub the marinade into the meat. Let chill for 2–3 hours.

3 Heat the remaining oil in a wok or large skillet and cook the duck, skin-side down, over medium heat for 3–4 minutes until the skin is browned and crisp and the meat cooked most of the way through.

4 Turn the breasts over and cook until browned and the meat is cooked to your liking.

5 Meanwhile, arrange the pineapple, cucumber, tomatoes, and onions on a platter. Mix the dressing ingredients together and pour over the top.

6 Lift the duck out of the wok and slice thickly. Arrange the duck slices on top of the salad and serve while still hot.

SERVES 4

4 boned duck breasts, skin on

1 lemon grass stalk, broken into three and each cut in
  half lengthwise

3 tbsp vegetable or peanut oil

2 tbsp sesame oil

1 tsp fish sauce

1 fresh green chile, seeded and chopped

2 tbsp Red Curry Paste (see page 31)

1/2 fresh pineapple, peeled and sliced*

3-inch/7.5-cm piece cucumber, peeled, seeded, and sliced

3 tomatoes, cut into wedges

1 onion, sliced thinly

for the dressing

juice of 1 lemon

2 garlic cloves, crushed

1 tsp jaggery or soft, light brown sugar

2 tbsp vegetable or peanut oil

cook's tip
You can set aside the pineapple leaves to use as
a garnish.

mixed seafood salad
yum ta-le

SERVES 4

3 tbsp vegetable or peanut oil

1 small onion, sliced thinly

8 oz/225 g baby squid, cleaned and sliced

8 oz/225 g cooked shrimp, shelled

1 lb/500 g mussels, unshelled

bunch of scallions, chopped coarsely

1 lemon grass stalk, chopped finely

1 red bell pepper, seeded and cut into strips

$\frac{1}{2}$ small head Napa cabbage, shredded

2 garlic cloves, crushed

1 tsp fish sauce

1 tsp jaggery or soft, light brown sugar

juice of 1 lemon

2-inch/5-cm piece cucumber, chopped

1 tomato, seeded and chopped

1 Heat 1 tablespoon of the oil in a wok or large skillet and stir-fry the onion, squid, shrimp, and mussels for 1–2 minutes, until the squid is opaque and the mussels have opened.

2 Mix the scallions, lemon grass, red bell pepper, and Napa cabbage together in a bowl. Add the seafood and stir gently. Turn into a serving dish.

3 Mix the garlic, the remaining oil, fish sauce, sugar, and lemon juice together. Add the chopped cucumber and tomato, spoon the dressing over the salad and seafood, and serve immediately.

Some Thai edifices are built on a vast scale

stir-fried vegetable salad
pahd puk

SERVES 4

4 tbsp vegetable or peanut oil

bunch of scallions, chopped

¹/₂ small cabbage (any variety), shredded

5 cups fresh spinach, washed

8 oz/225 g bok choy, halved or quartered
  if necessary

6 oz/175 g Chinese or purple sprouting broccoli

1 small head Napa cabbage, shredded

few sprigs Thai basil

2 fresh red chiles, seeded and chopped

2 tbsp oyster sauce

1 tsp jaggery or soft, light brown sugar

1 tbsp sesame oil

2 tbsp sesame seeds, toasted

1 Heat 2 tablespoons of oil in a wok or large skillet and sauté the scallions, all the leaves, basil, and chiles quickly until just wilted. Transfer to a serving plate.

2 Mix the oyster sauce, sugar, remaining vegetable oil, and sesame oil together and pour over the leaves.

3 Sprinkle the sesame seeds over the top and serve immediately.

Elegance is important to both architecture and cuisine

angler fish salad
yum pla

SERVES 4

1 lb/450 g angler fish, skinned and boned

juice of 1 lime

3 tbsp vegetable or peanut oil

$^1/_2$ tsp fish sauce

2 fresh red chiles, seeded and sliced

generous $^1/_2$ cup all-purpose flour

oil, for cooking

1 romaine lettuce, torn into pieces

$^1/_4$ white cabbage, shredded

1 small onion, sliced thinly

for the dressing

juice of 1 lime

1 tsp jaggery or soft, light brown sugar

1 tsp fish sauce

handful of fresh cilantro, chopped

1 Cut the fish into even-size cubes, each about 1 inch/2.5 cm and put into a shallow dish. Mix the lime juice, oil, fish sauce, and chiles together and pour over the fish. Cover, let chill, and let marinate for 1–2 hours.

2 Put the flour onto a plate. Lift the fish out of the marinade and roll the pieces in the flour. Heat the oil in a wok or large skillet and cook the fish, in batches if necessary, until browned all over. Lift out and drain on paper towels.

3 Put the lettuce, cabbage, and onion on a serving platter and arrange the fish on top.

4 Mix the dressing ingredients together and pour over the whole salad. Serve immediately while the fish is still warm.

tomato and squid salad
yum pla-muek

SERVES 4

1 lb/450 g tomatoes

1 lb/450 g baby squid, cleaned and left whole

2 garlic cloves, chopped finely

2 fresh green chiles, seeded and sliced

handful of fresh cilantro, chopped

juice of 1 lime

1 tsp fish sauce

1 tbsp Thai soy sauce

1 Peel the tomatoes (see page 24). Cut into quarters, remove all the seeds, and discard them. Finely chop the tomato flesh and set aside.

2 Bring a medium pan of water to a boil, add the squid and their tentacles and cook for 2–3 minutes. Remove and drain well.

3 Mix the tomatoes, garlic, chiles, and half the cilantro. Add the squid, and toss everything together. Turn into a serving dish.

4 Mix the lime juice, fish and soy sauces, and the remaining cilantro. Pour the dressing over the salad. Serve warm or cold.

Sculpture and intricate decoration are key elements of Thai art

crab and cilantro salad
yum pue

SERVES 4

12 oz/350 g canned white crabmeat, drained

4 scallions, finely chopped

handful of fresh cilantro, chopped

for the dressing

1 garlic clove, crushed

1-inch/2.5-cm piece gingerroot, peeled and grated

2 lime leaves, torn into pieces

juice of 1 lime

1 tsp fish sauce

1 iceberg lettuce, shredded

3-inch/7.5-cm piece cucumber, chopped

1 Put the crabmeat into a bowl and stir in the scallions and cilantro.

2 Mix the ingredients for the dressing together.

3 Place the lettuce leaves on a serving platter and sprinkle with the cucumber.

4 Arrange the crab salad over the leaves and drizzle the dressing over the salad. Serve immediately.

Buddhist monks in their saffron-colored robes are an integral part of society in Thailand

peppered beef salad
yum nuea

SERVES 4

4 x 4 oz/115 g fillet steaks

2 tbsp black peppercorns, crushed

1 tsp Chinese five spice powder

³/₄ cup bean sprouts

1-inch/2.5-cm piece gingerroot, chopped finely

4 shallots, sliced finely

1 red bell pepper, seeded and sliced thinly

3 tbsp Thai soy sauce

2 fresh red chiles, seeded and sliced

¹/₂ lemon grass stalk, chopped finely

3 tbsp vegetable or peanut oil

1 tbsp sesame oil

1 Wash the steaks and pat dry on paper towels. Mix the peppercorns with the five spice and press onto all sides of the steaks. Cook on a grill pan or under a broiler for 2–3 minutes each side, or until cooked to your liking.

2 Meanwhile mix the bean sprouts, half the ginger, the shallots, and bell pepper together and divide between 4 plates. Mix the remaining ginger, soy sauce, chiles, lemon grass, and oils together.

3 Slice the beef and arrange on the vegetables. Drizzle with the dressing and serve immediately.

Salad ingredients are bought daily in Thai markets

hot-and-sour vegetable salad
yum puk

SERVES 4

2 tbsp vegetable or peanut oil

1 tbsp chili oil

1 onion, sliced

1-inch/2.5-cm piece gingerroot, grated

1 small head broccoli, cut into florets

2 carrots, cut into short thin sticks

1 red bell pepper, seeded and cut into squares

1 yellow bell pepper, seeded and cut into strips

2 oz/55 g snow peas, trimmed and halved

2 oz/55 g baby corn, halved

for the dressing

2 tbsp vegetable or peanut oil

1 tsp chili oil

1 tbsp rice wine vinegar

juice of 1 lime

$^1/_2$ tsp fish sauce

1 Heat the oils in a wok or large skillet and sauté the onion and ginger for 1–2 minutes until they start to soften. Add the vegetables and stir-fry for 2–3 minutes until they have softened slightly. Remove from the heat and set aside.

2 Mix the dressing ingredients together. Transfer the vegetables to a serving plate and drizzle the dressing over. Serve warm immediately, or let the flavors develop and serve cold.

Right *Thai families earn great merit when a son takes up the monk's robe*

Overleaf *Chiles are essential to many classic Thai dishes, and are used to flavor oil and dipping sauce*

sea bass and mango salad
yum mamuang seabass

SERVES 2

2 small sea bass, cleaned

1 tbsp Red Curry Paste (see page 31)

small handful of fresh cilantro, chopped

²/₃ cup coconut milk

2 tbsp sweet chili sauce

6–8 Thai basil leaves, chopped

¹/₂ tsp fish sauce

1 tsp rice wine vinegar

1 mango, seeded, peeled, and sliced

selection of mixed salad greens

1 Place the fish on a board. Mix the curry paste and cilantro together and stuff inside each fish cavity. Cover and let marinate for 1–2 hours.

2 Preheat the oven to 400°F/200°C. Place the fish in a roasting pan. Mix the coconut milk, chili sauce, basil, fish sauce, and vinegar, and pour over the fish. Arrange the mango slices in the pan as well. Cover with foil and cook for 15 minutes.

3 Remove the foil and cook uncovered for an additional 10–15 minutes until cooked.

4 Place the fish on 2 warmed serving plates, drizzle with the cooking sauces, and serve with the mixed salad greens.

An abundance of fresh fish is available in Thailand's markets

red chicken salad
yum ped daeng

SERVES 4

4 boned chicken breasts

2 tbsp Red Curry Paste (see page 31)

2 tbsp vegetable or peanut oil

1 head Napa cabbage, shredded

6 oz/175 g bok choy, torn into large pieces

½ savoy cabbage, shredded

2 shallots, chopped finely

2 garlic cloves, crushed

1 tbsp rice wine vinegar

2 tbsp sweet chili sauce

2 tbsp Thai soy sauce

1 Slash the flesh of the chicken several times and rub the curry paste into each cut. Cover and let chill overnight.

2 Cook in a heavy-bottom pan over medium heat or on a grill pan for 5-6 minutes, turning once or twice, until cooked through. Keep warm.

3 Heat 1 tablespoon of the oil in a wok or large skillet and stir-fry the leaves, bok choy, and cabbage until just wilted. Add the remaining oil, shallots, and garlic, and stir-fry until just tender but not browned. Add the vinegar, chili sauce, and soy. Remove from the heat.

4 Arrange the leaves on 4 serving plates. Slice the chicken, arrange on the salad greens, and drizzle the hot dressing over. Serve immediately.

Lemon grass is a popular ingredient that adds a distinctive flavor to salads, soups, and sauces

shrimp and papaya salad
somtam gung

SERVES 4

1 papaya, peeled

12 oz/350 g large cooked shrimp, shelled

for the dressing

4 scallions, chopped finely

2 fresh red chiles, seeded and chopped finely

1 tsp fish sauce

1 tbsp vegetable or peanut oil

juice of 1 lime

1 tsp jaggery or soft, light brown sugar

assorted baby green salad greens

1 Scoop the seeds out of the papaya and slice thinly. Stir gently together with the shrimp.

2 Mix the scallions, chiles, fish sauce, oil, lime juice, and sugar together.

3 Arrange the salad greens in a bowl and top with the papaya and shrimp. Pour the dressing over and serve immediately.

A trip to a Thai market can provide a friendly discussion and an array of salad items

curried egg salad
yum khai

SERVES 4

6 eggs

1 tbsp vegetable or peanut oil

1 onion, chopped

1 tbsp Yellow Curry Paste (see page 93)

4 tbsp plain yogurt

¹/₂ tsp salt

handful of fresh cilantro, chopped finely

bunch of watercress or arugula

2 zucchinis, cut into short thin sticks

1 fresh green chile, seeded and chopped finely

1 tsp fish sauce

1 tsp rice wine vinegar

3 tbsp vegetable or peanut oil

1 Put the eggs in a pan, cover with cold water, and bring to a boil. Let simmer for 10 minutes, then drain and rinse in cold water. Shell and halve.

2 Meanwhile, heat the oil in a medium skillet and sauté the onion gently until softened but not browned. Remove from the heat and stir in the curry paste. Let cool slightly before stirring in the yogurt, salt, and half the cilantro. Set aside.

3 Arrange the watercress and zucchinis on a platter. Mix the chile, fish sauce, vinegar, and oil together and pour the dressing over the leaves.

4 Arrange the eggs on top and spoon the yogurt mixture over each one. Garnish with the remaining cilantro over the top and serve immediately.

gingered chicken and vegetable salad
yum gai khing

SERVES 4

4 skinned, boned chicken breasts

4 scallions, chopped

1-inch/2.5-cm piece gingerroot, chopped finely

2 garlic cloves, crushed

2 tbsp vegetable or peanut oil

for the salad

1 tbsp vegetable or peanut oil

1 onion, sliced

2 garlic cloves, chopped

4 oz/115 g baby corn, halved

4 oz/115 g snow peas, halved lengthwise

1 red bell pepper, seeded and sliced

3-inch/7.5-cm piece cucumber, peeled,
  seeded, and sliced

4 tbsp Thai soy sauce

1 tbsp jaggery or soft, light brown sugar

few Thai basil leaves

6 oz/175 g fine egg noodles

1 Cut the chicken into large cubes, each about 1 inch/2.5 cm. Mix the scallions, ginger, garlic, and oil together in a shallow dish and add the chicken. Cover and let marinate for at least 3 hours. Lift the meat out of the marinade and set aside.

2 Heat the oil in a wok or large skillet and cook the onion for 1–2 minutes before adding the rest of the vegetables except the cucumber. Cook for 2–3 minutes, until just tender. Add the cucumber, half the soy sauce, the sugar, and basil, and mix gently.

3 Soak the noodles for 2–3 minutes (check the package instructions) or until tender and drain well. Sprinkle the remaining soy sauce over them and arrange on plates. Top with the cooked vegetables.

4 Add a little more oil to the wok if necessary and cook the chicken over fairly high heat until browned on all sides. Arrange the chicken cubes on top of the salad and serve hot or warm.

julienne vegetable salad
yum puk foi

SERVES 4

4 tbsp vegetable or peanut oil

8 oz/225 g tofu with herbs, cubed

1 red onion, sliced

4 scallions, cut into 2-inch/5-cm lengths

1 garlic clove, chopped

2 carrots, cut into short thin sticks

4 oz/115 g fine green beans, trimmed

1 yellow bell pepper, seeded and cut into strips

4 oz/115 g broccoli, cut into florets

1 large zucchini, cut into short thin sticks

³/₈ cup bean sprouts

2 tbsp Red Curry Paste (see page 31)

4 tbsp Thai soy sauce

1 tbsp rice wine vinegar

1 tsp jaggery or soft, light brown sugar

few Thai basil leaves

12 oz/350 g rice vermicelli noodles

1 Heat the oil in a wok or large skillet and cook the tofu cubes for 3–4 minutes, until browned on all sides. Lift out of the oil and drain on paper towels.

2 Add the onions, garlic, and carrots to the hot oil and cook for 1–2 minutes before adding the rest of the vegetables, except for the bean sprouts. Stir-fry for 2–3 minutes. Add the bean sprouts, then stir in the curry paste, soy, vinegar, sugar, and basil leaves. Cook for 30 seconds.

3 Soak the noodles in boiling water or stock for 2–3 minutes (check the package instructions) or until tender and drain well.

4 Pile the vegetables onto the noodles, and serve topped with the tofu cubes. Garnish with extra basil if liked.

eggplant and onion salad
yum makuea

This looks attractive made with an assortment of eggplant varieties. No matter what you use, make sure they are all cut to the same size.

SERVES 4

4 tbsp vegetable or peanut oil

1 onion, sliced

4 shallots, chopped finely

4 scallions, sliced

12 oz/350 g eggplants, cubed

2 tbsp Green Curry Paste (see page 31)

2 tbsp Thai soy sauce

1 tsp jaggery or soft, light brown sugar

4 oz/115 g block creamed coconut, chopped

3 tbsp water

small handful of fresh cilantro, chopped

few Thai basil leaves, chopped

small handful of fresh parsley, chopped

2¹/₂ cups arugula leaves

2 tbsp sweet chili sauce

1 Heat half the oil in a wok or large skillet and cook all the onions together for 1–2 minutes, until just softened but not browned. Lift out and set aside.

2 Cook the eggplant cubes, in batches if necessary, adding more oil as necessary, until they are crisp and golden brown.

3 Return the onions to the wok and add the curry paste, soy sauce, and sugar. Add the creamed coconut and water and cook until dissolved. Stir in most of the cilantro, the basil, and parsley.

4 Toss the arugula in the chili sauce and serve with the eggplant and onion salad. Garnish with the remaining herbs.

DESSERTS

This last section of the book is a bit of a cheat. Thai people don't really eat the same sort of desserts at home as we do in the West. They might have fresh fruit or tapioca, or dumplings made from mung bean flour, but having no dairy products means no cream, chocolate, or cheesecakes. This might sound disappointing to sweet-toothed people, but it needn't be.

I know people who look at the dessert menu first, decide how much space they need to leave for their dessert and adjust their other courses accordingly. So I had to find a way round this potential drawback to the Thai menu. Dumplings with red bean jelly in the center may not appeal to many Western palates—we tend to want something sweeter and more familiar and need to find ways to combine Thailand's produce to make everyone happy. It's actually turned out to be very easy, as the flavors, spices, and fruit of the country lend themselves to lots of different desserts that we in the West can instantly recognize.

After all the exciting, spicy flavors of one or two first courses, our taste buds may well need something to calm them down. So I have majored on those desserts which combine some of the wonderful fruit and nuts that are sold in colorful abundance in the markets in Thailand with some of the sweeter spices to complete the Thai experience.

You don't need any specialist equipment, just a whisk, ramekins, and the usual range of pans and skillets. There is an ice cream recipe, as well as one for a pineapple and lime sherbet, so if you have an ice-cream maker, these desserts would be ideal and straightforward to prepare. However, as I suspect most of us don't have one of these machines, these two freezer desserts will have to be made in the more traditional way.

Thailand produces coconuts, pineapples, and bananas, and the more exotic litchis and pomelos. These fruits are varied in flavor and texture—and deliciously versatile. Bananas can be mashed, or barbecued, or sliced into salads. (Toss them in lime or lemon juice once peeled, as they discolor quickly.) The easiest way to peel a pineapple is to cut off the leafy top and base, cut it into thick slices, and then trim away the tough skin with a sharp knife. If the fruit is ripe, the core will be soft enough to eat; if not, cut it out and discard. If you want to use fresh coconut, here's a good way to open it. Use a hammer to tap round the center of the shell. Keep tapping and turning and eventually the shell will crack in half. (Hold it over a bowl while you do this to catch the liquid once the nut cracks open.)

the flavors, spices, and fruit...lend themselves to lots of different desserts that we...can recognize

I have used spices, such as ginger and cinnamon, in combination with these fruits to make the best use of Thailand's great flavors. Ground ginger and cinnamon are widely available. Balls of preserved ginger covered with syrup can be chopped into ice creams or cakes, or sliced and used to decorate creamy desserts and fools. Cinnamon sticks added to simmering milk provide extra flavor (discard them before serving or freezing). Both of these should be available in supermarkets, grocers, or delicatessens.

You will never find this type of dessert in Thailand or a Thai restaurant, as Thais simply do not eat this type of food. These recipes have been created to combine the traditional flavors of this beautiful country with Western contemporary expectations of what makes a good dessert.

banana and coconut ice cream
i tim ma-prown sai khuay

SERVES 6–8

3 oz/85 g block creamed coconut, chopped

2¹/₂ cups heavy cream

¹/₂ cup confectioners' sugar

2 bananas

1 tsp lemon juice

fresh fruit, to serve

1 Put the creamed coconut in a small bowl. Add just enough boiling water to cover and stir until dissolved. Let cool.

2 Whip the cream with the confectioners' sugar until thick but still floppy*. Mash the bananas with the lemon juice and whisk gently into the cream together with the cold coconut.

3 Transfer to a freezerproof container and freeze overnight. Serve in scoops with fresh fruit.

cook's tip

Take care not to overwhip the cream or it will curdle when the other ingredients are added.

The highly prized lotus flower

creamy mango brûlée
mamuang

1 Slice the mangoes on either side of the seed. Discard the seed and peel the fruit. Slice and then chop the fruit. Divide it between 4 ramekins.

2 Beat the mascarpone cheese with the yogurt. Fold in the ginger, lime rind and juice, and soft brown sugar. Divide the mixture between the ramekins and level off the tops. Let chill for 2 hours.

3 Sprinkle 2 tablespoons of raw brown sugar over the top of each dish, covering the creamy mixture. Place under a hot broiler for 2–3 minutes, until melted and browned. Let cool, then let chill until required. This dessert should be eaten on the day of making.

SERVES 4

2 mangoes

generous 1 cup mascarpone cheese

generous 3/4 cup strained plain yogurt

1 tsp ground ginger

grated rind and juice of 1 lime

2 tbsp soft, light brown sugar

8 tbsp raw brown sugar

Some of the images of Buddha are made of solid gold

spicy rice pudding
kau mun

1 Put the coconut milk and milk in a pan and heat gently. Add the sugar and stir until it has dissolved.

2 Add the rice and spice and gradually bring to a boil. Let simmer gently, stirring frequently, for 45–60 minutes, until thickened.

3 Stir in the butter and once it has melted, serve immediately, sprinkled with cinnamon.

SERVES 4

1³/₄ cups canned coconut milk

²/₃ cup milk

generous ¹/₄ cup soft brown sugar

generous ¹/₄ cup short-grain rice

2 tsp allspice

1 oz/25 g butter

1 tsp ground cinnamon

*The rivers and canals
of the central plain are
its peaceful highways*

pineapple and lime sherbet
subparot, ma-nau i tim

SERVES 4

generous 1 cup superfine sugar

2¹/₂ cups water

grated rind and juice of 2 limes

1 small pineapple, peeled, quartered, and chopped*

sweet cookies, to serve

*cook's tip

You can also halve the pineapple, cut out the flesh, and use the shell as an attractive way of serving the sherbet.

1 Put the sugar and water into a pan and heat gently, stirring until the sugar has dissolved. Bring to a boil and let simmer for 10 minutes.

2 Stir in the grated rind and half the lime juice. Remove from the heat and let cool.

3 Put the pineapple in a blender or food processor and process until smooth. Add to the cold syrup with the remaining lime juice. Pour into a freezerproof container and freeze until crystals have formed round the edge.

4 Turn out the sherbet into a bowl. Beat well with a fork to break up the crystals. Return to the freezer and chill overnight. Serve in scoops with sweet cookies.

The night sky in Thailand is lit up with the distinctive shapes of its shrines and temples

mixed fruit salad
polamai ruam

SERVES 4

1 papaya, halved, peeled, and seeded

2 bananas, sliced thickly

1 small pineapple, peeled, halved, cored, and sliced

12 litchis, peeled

1 small melon, seeded and cut into thin wedges

2 oranges

grated rind and juice of 1 lime

2 tbsp superfine sugar

1 Arrange the papaya, bananas, pineapple, litchis, and melon on a serving platter. Cut off the rind and pith from the oranges. Cut the orange slices out from between the membranes and add to the fruit platter. Grate a small quantity of the discarded orange rind and add to the platter.

2 Combine the lime rind, juice, and sugar. Pour over the salad and serve.

mini coconut crêpes
kanum buang ma-prow oon

SERVES 4

2 oz/55 g block creamed coconut, chopped

$^2/_3$ cup boiling water

1$^1/_2$ cups all-purpose flour

2 tbsp superfine sugar

2 eggs

generous 1$^3/_4$ cups milk

$^1/_4$ cup dry unsweetened coconut

2 oz/55 g butter

$^1/_2$ melon, seeded, peeled, and sliced thinly

1 Put the creamed coconut in a bowl, pour in the measured water, and stir until dissolved.

2 Sift the flour in another bowl and stir in the sugar. Beat in the eggs and half the milk. Gradually beat in the remaining milk and then the coconut mixture to make a creamy batter. Stir in the unsweetened coconut.

3 Melt a little of the butter in a heavy-bottom skillet. Add 3–4 tablespoons of the batter, spacing them well apart as they will spread during cooking. Cook for 1–2 minutes, then flip over to cook the second side. Remove from the skillet and keep warm. Cook the remaining batter in the same way. Serve warm with melon slices.

Overleaf *Shrines and temples are sometimes in isolated or wooded areas. Treat any sacred place with great respect*

banana-stuffed crêpes
pang ho khuay

SERVES 4

1¹/₂ cups all-purpose flour

2 tbsp soft, light brown sugar

2 eggs

generous 1³/₄ cups milk

grated rind and juice of 1 lemon

2 oz/55 g butter

3 bananas

4 tbsp golden syrup

1 Combine the flour and sugar and beat in the eggs and half the milk. Beat together until smooth. Gradually add the remaining milk, stirring constantly to make a smooth batter. Stir in the lemon rind.

2 Melt a little butter in an 8-inch/20-cm skillet and pour in one-quarter of the batter. Tilt the skillet to coat the bottom and cook for 1–2 minutes, until set. Flip the crêpe over and cook the second side. Slide out of the skillet and keep warm. Repeat to make 3 more crêpes.

3 Slice the bananas and toss in the lemon juice. Pour the syrup over them and toss together. Fold each crêpe into 4 and fill the center with the banana mixture. Serve warm.

A close-up of the ornamental decoration on a roof support

roasted spicy pineapple
subparot ob

SERVES 4

1 pineapple

1 mango, peeled, seeded, and sliced

2 oz/55 g butter

4 tbsp golden syrup

1-2 tsp cinnamon

1 tsp freshly grated nutmeg

4 tbsp soft brown sugar

2 passion fruit

$^2/_3$ cup sour cream

finely grated rind of 1 orange

1 Preheat the oven to 400°F/200°C. Use a sharp knife to cut off the top, base, and skin of the pineapple, then cut into quarters. Remove the central core and cut the flesh into large cubes. Place them in a roasting pan with the mango.

2 Place the butter, syrup, cinnamon, nutmeg, and sugar in a small pan and heat gently, stirring constantly, until melted. Pour the mixture over the fruit. Roast for 20–30 minutes, until the fruit is browned.

3 Halve the passion fruit and scoop out the seeds. Spoon over the roasted fruit. Mix the sour cream and orange rind together and serve with the fruit.

1 Put the creamed coconut and cream in a small pan and heat gently until the coconut has dissolved. Remove from the heat and set aside to cool for 10 minutes, then whisk until thick but floppy.

2 Peel the bananas and toss in the lime juice and rind. Lightly oil a preheated grill pan and cook the bananas, turning once, for 2–3 minutes, until soft and browned.

3 Toast the dry unsweetened coconut on a piece of foil under a broiler until lightly browned. Serve the bananas with the coconut cream, sprinkled with the toasted coconut.

griddled bananas
khuay ping

251

SERVES 4

2 oz/55 g block creamed coconut, chopped

$^2/_3$ cup heavy cream

4 bananas

juice and rind of 1 lime

1 tbsp vegetable or peanut oil

scant $^1/_2$ cup dry unsweetened coconut

ginger creams and sesame pastries
ka-num rung ob yha rad na khing

1 Whip the cream until thick but not floppy. Stir in the yogurt and the ginger syrup. Divide the preserved ginger between 4 glasses or cups and then top with the ginger cream. Sprinkle 1 tablespoon of sugar on each one and let chill overnight.

2 Preheat the oven to 400°F/200°C. Cut the phyllo pastry into 16 x 4-inch/10-cm squares. Brush 1 square with melted butter, then place another square on top. Repeat twice more to make a 4-layered pastry. Make 3 more in the same way.

3 Brush with butter and sprinkle with sesame seeds and bake for 10–15 minutes, until golden brown. Serve warm with the ginger creams.

SERVES 4

generous 1³/₄ cups heavy cream

²/₃ cup plain yogurt

4 tbsp ginger syrup (from the preserved ginger jar)

6 pieces preserved ginger, chopped

4 tbsp soft brown sugar

4 oz/115 g phyllo pastry

2 oz/55 g butter, melted

3 tbsp sesame seeds

Thailand boasts paradise beaches as well as vibrant cities

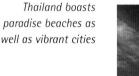